EARLY CHILDHOOD EDUCATION SERIES

Leslie R. Williams, Editor   Millie Almy, Senior Advisor

ADVISORY BOARD: Barbara T. Bowman, Harriet K. Cuffaro, Stephanie Feeney,
Doris Pronin Fromberg, Celia Genishi, Stacie G. Goffin, Dominic F. Gullo,
Alice Sterling Honig, Elizabeth Jones, Gwen Morgan, David Weikart

---

(Continued)

Bringing
Reggio Emilia
Home

AN INNOVATIVE APPROACH TO
EARLY CHILDHOOD EDUCATION

LOUISE BOYD CADWELL

FOREWORD BY LELLA GANDINI

TEACHERS COLLEGE PRESS

Teachers College, Columbia University
New York and London

Cover drawing by Jessica Ahnet

Photography and chapter opening artwork by Louise Boyd Cadwell

Published by Teachers College Press, 1234 Amsterdam Avenue, New York, NY 10027

Copyright © 1997 by Teachers College, Columbia University

All rights reserved. No part of this publication may be reproduced or transmitted in any form or by any means, electronic or mechanical, including photocopy, or any information storage and retrieval system, without permission from the publisher.

Library of Congress Cataloging-in-Publication Data

Cadwell, Louise Boyd.
    Bringing Reggio Emilia home : an innovative approach to early childhood education / Louise Boyd Cadwell ; foreword by Lella Gandini.
      p.   cm. — (Early childhood education series)
    Includes bibliographical references (p.   ) and index.
    ISBN 0-8077-3661-9 (cloth : alk. paper). — ISBN 0-8077-3660-0 (pbk. : alk. paper)
    1. Education, Preschool—Philosophy.   2. Early childhood education—Philosophy.   3. Education, Preschool—Italy—Reggio Emilia.   I. Title. II. Series.
    LB1140.3.C23   1997
    372.21'01—dc21   97-17760

ISBN 0-8077-3660-0 (paper)
ISBN 0-8077-3661-9 (cloth)

Printed on acid-free paper
Manufactured in the United States of America

04 03 02 01 00 99 98   8 7 6 5 4 3 2

For my parents, Adeline and Ingram Boyd,
my children, Alden and Christopher,
and my husband, Ashley

Contents

Foreword

This book, the narrative of a personal journey, results from experiences under-gone during a specific historical phase in the development of the program for young children in Reggio Emilia, and in the growth of interest in that program in the United States. Between 1989 and 1993, just three educators from the United States were granted permission to spend a year as interns in the schools of Reggio. Louise Cadwell was one of them, and her year there was 1991–92. Later, in 1993, as requests by foreign educators to learn about the Reggio Emilia approach and to visit the schools there continually increased exponentially, and as Reggio Children was established as an organization to support the dissemina-tion of the Reggio Emilia approach, such internships were severely curtailed. From then on, educators coming from abroad would be granted only short stays, and these for specific, selected goals in harmony with coherent plans of dissemination. The opportunity for a one-year internship in Reggio turned out to be unique for Louise Cadwell, as well as for the other two interns, Baji Rankin and Eva Tarini.

In 1992 I met with Louise Cadwell several times in Reggio, especially during the months in which she was doing her internship at La Villetta School, as I returned often to do research there during the spring. As it happened, listening to Louise's perspective as she was sorting out her reflections on the powerful experience she was having at Reggio was a good way to learn about the work of the teachers and the children there. At that time she was specifically interested in learning about the ways children express themselves through many different art materials, and through spoken and written language when they are involved in rich and meaningful experiences, especially experiences close to the natural world. Louise expressed her intention, once back in the United States, to write a book on this topic; this book has gone far beyond her initial intention. A journal about the development of concepts and practices of education, it is a narrative of two very different but connected educational experiences, one in Reggio Emilia and one in St. Louis. She begins with a captivating personal ac-count of her preparation for the encounter with Reggio Emilia and its schools. The following two parts of the book are both essential for giving a new perspec-tive on understanding the Reggio Emilia approach. Each of these two parts depends on the other. Louise's account of her internship in the schools shows the observant and reflective path of a learner who is taking in events and infor-mation and interpreting them. Then the narrative about the changes in the school in St. Louis, where she was deeply engaged in trying to translate what she had learned in Reggio into the life of the classrooms there, relates her account of becoming actively aware of the meaning of what she had observed.

With regard to the first part of the book, I am particularly grateful to Louise for transcribing for us Vea Vecchi's words and thoughts. These transcripts bring to us stories of children and teachers involved in engaging projects that we could not easily have witnessed. Her description, in poetic and sensitive prose, of Vea and Marina Mori, another teacher at Diana School, and the transcripts of dialogues with children reveal a great deal about the importance of relationship. We watch the relationship between *atelierista* and teacher, among teachers, and among children. We also see unfolding the children's understanding about the relationships among people and things in our world.

Yet, the description of what happens at the Diana School conveys a sense of effortless gliding through the school days, in and out of experiences and conversations where the aesthetic aspects prevail as an "exquisite dance." What we do not see is what makes it possible to work with such concentration and pleasure; we do not see the hard work, the carefully orchestrated organization, or the participation by educators, staff, and parents. We do not see the difficulties of negotiation and collaboration, or the connection with various parts of the system.

It is the second part of the book, containing the beginning and evolution of the work in St. Louis, that illustrates the complexity of what Louise had admired so much in Reggio. When Louise describes her role of consultant and *atelierista* in collaboration with other St. Louis educators, and starts to adapt the ideas from Reggio Emilia in St. Louis, she examines the difficulties and issues that she had not understood. Gradually she describes how, with other teachers, and with the support of Amelia Gambetti sent by Reggio Children, they became aware of the connectedness of all the parts of the system: space, materials, organization, collaboration among colleagues, and participation by parents. They realize how everything contributes to making it possible to really listen to children and to start to work in a truly different way.

Louise's journey started as a quest for meaning of the extraordinary way that children express themselves in the experiences and projects in the schools of Reggio Emilia. It continued in the awareness that she had extended her discovery of the power of the connecting web when many positive relationships are activated and nurtured. Now, in St. Louis, the journey of Louise Cadwell continues as a shared experience toward a deeper understanding of the potential of children and adults, constructing a network that sustains their mutual conversation in many languages.

Lella Gandini

Acknowledgments

I am grateful to the educators, children, and parents of the preschools of Reggio Emilia, Italy, who inspired this work and made it possible through their kindness, patience, and openness. I wish to thank Carlina Rinaldi, Sergio Spaggiari, and the late Loris Malaguzzi specifically, for allowing me to be an intern in their preschools and for offering me their continual support both while I was in Reggio Emilia and after I returned to the United States. The educators and staff of the Diana and La Villetta Schools were particularly kind and generous in helping me to understand their ways of working as I lived beside them day-to-day in their schools. I wish to thank my colleagues in Reggio Emilia for granting me permission to use my journal notes, recorded, transcribed conversations, photographs taken in the schools, and copies of children's drawings in this book.

Carlina Rinaldi, Vea Vecchi, Marina Mori, Amelia Gambetti, Giovanni Piazza, and Mara Davoli continue to be colleagues and mentors to me as I work to understand and adapt the Reggio Approach in my own country. It is due to Amelia's help that we have come as far as we have in our work in St. Louis.

Equal tribute and grateful thanks go to the educators, children, and parents of the College School of Webster Groves, who, in the adventurous spirit on which the school is based, took the risk of inviting major change and innovation into their early childhood classrooms. In particular, I want to thank Director Jan Phillips for her unfailing support through the many challenges we have faced together.

My team of colleagues in the preschool have been my partners in the effort to go ever deeper in understanding and adapting the Reggio Approach at the College School. Dorris Roberts has helped me to slow down and think before making too many changes too fast. Joyce Devlin has inspired all of us by her flexibility and skill in making enormous changes in the way she works in the last years of her career. Jennifer Strange has pushed us all to continue to uncover what true collaboration means. These three women have been essential contributors to the stories told in this book.

Honey Norlander, Kathy Seibel, and Skylar Harmann worked with me to carry the work of adaptation of the Reggio Approach beyond the preschool and I am grateful to them for that opportunity. Student teachers Nancy Nistler and Becky Cornwall were an invaluable help in documenting stories which might otherwise have slipped by all of us.

The work at the College School might never have begun without the vision and dedication of several parents. After seeing the exhibit, "The Hundred Languages of Children," in St. Louis, Courtney and Gyo Obata, Nita van der Werff, Nancy Klepper, and Lucia May made it possible for a group of five College School representatives to visit the Reggio Emilia preschools in the spring of

1992. Parent architects Gay and Frank Lorberbaum worked with us to design and build our new spaces. Along with these parents, countless others have supported our collective work in the understanding and practice of an approach which is both a challenge and a gift for all of us.

From the beginning, Brenda Fyfe of Webster University has been a colleague and friend. Many times, her partnership has steadied us when the side effects of change threatened our progress. Lori Geismar Ryan of the Clayton Schools' Family Center has offered us all her ability to think and write clearly as well as her strengths in the analysis and interpretation of both the large issues and the small details involved in this kind of change. I thank Chuck Schwall, *atelierista* at the St. Michael School, for his willingness to tackle difficult questions about our roles as *atelieristi* and to collaborate with me as we discover the complexity of our work.

This book would never have been written without the inspiration and practical guidance of John Elder, who insisted that I write it in a strong, lively, narrative voice and then showed me how. I am grateful to John for introducing me to authors Scott Russell Sanders, Ann Zwinger, Gary Paul Nabhan, and Steven Trimble. Among others, these nature writers have opened my eyes to the intricate beauty of the natural world and to the wonder and power that words hold in the telling of stories.

Judith Burton has held me to high standards throughout work on two degrees. I am grateful for her sound knowledge and deep understanding of child development through the arts. John Elder, Judith Burton, Ellen Colburn, Joe Meeker, David Marsters, and Gail Wheeler were all members of my doctoral committee as I worked toward my degree at the Union Institute. I am grateful to all of them for their constancy and their specific help with many aspects of my work.

I am indebted to Jeanne Goldhaber of the University of Vermont, who was a dedicated reader and helpful editor of every draft of this book. My good friend and fellow educator, Rena Diana, also contributed her fine editing skills and valuable insights to the manuscript. Lella Gandini has been a great help to me both as a reader and as a liaison with the educators in Reggio Emilia. Susan Liddicoat of Teachers College Press has been a most patient and skillful editor.

Along with being readers and editors, both my husband, Ashley Cadwell and my mother, Adeline Boyd, have provided all the moral and practical support that was necessary for me to write day after day. Finally, I wish to thank my children, Alden and Christopher, and all the children I have known, for helping me to live close to childhood and to wonder.

Prologue

This book is a collection of stories based on my experience as a teacher and my evolution as a researcher from 1991 to 1996. During this time, I journeyed to Italy and returned home again, always in passionate pursuit of settings and approaches that would inspire the best in young children's development through arts, language, and nature education. Throughout this period, my keen interest has been, and continues to be, the language children use and the symbols they make as they seek to build relationships with each other, with adults, and with the natural world. The collection of stories is composed of two parts. The first focuses on my experience as an intern in the municipally funded preschools of Reggio Emilia, Italy, and is told in Chapters 1, 2, and 3. The second, comprising Chapters 4, 5, and 6, is based on attempts to adapt what is known internationally as "The Reggio Approach," in the preschool and kindergarten classrooms of the College School, a private, independent school in St. Louis, Missouri.

The College School is one of 10 public and private schools from diverse settings in St. Louis city and county that were supported by the Danforth Foundation to study and begin to adapt the Reggio Approach from 1992 to 1995. These schools were selected because of the administrators', teachers', and parents' strong commitment to early childhood education and to the philosophy of the Reggio Approach. Some of the schools were more successful than others in sustaining the effort required in this kind of educational innovation. In *Teachers' Perceptions of a Pedagogic Innovation: Barriers and Mechanisms for Successful Implementation*, Entsminger (1994) concludes her study with a discussion of the teachers' understanding of some of the conditions that seemed essential to the initial efforts to adapt the Reggio Approach in these 10 schools. These included the strong support of the administration, the teachers' willingness to grapple with challenging issues involved in the theory and practice of teaching and learning, and the commitment of a group of teachers to meet on a regular basis to review and encourage each other's efforts in a collaborative context.

When the grant program ended in the spring of 1995, it was clear to those of us who administered it and to consultants from Reggio Emilia that 3 of the 10 schools had made significant, visible progress in understanding how the fundamentals of the approach could take root in their programs. These schools are the College School of Webster Groves, the St. Michael School, both of which are private and independent, and the Family Center, the school district of Clayton's early childhood and parent support program.

The College School will be discussed later in the prologue as it is the site of much of the work described in this book. The St. Michael School is a 26-year-old Episcopal school for children of all faiths serving 110 children from preschool through sixth grade. Over the past 20 years, Clayton Schools' Family Center has evolved into a multifaceted family support and resource program serving more than 400 families a year.

The teachers from these schools form a strong network. We continue to meet monthly as a whole group and more often in smaller groups to share our work and to support each other's growth. We observe in each other's class-rooms and act as peer coaches for one another. We invite outside experts into our schools to challenge us and to consult with us. Throughout our adaptation efforts we have worked for short but intense periods with Amelia Gambetti, consultant to schools in the United States for the international organization, Reggio Children. We also have continued to travel to Reggio Emilia to renew ourselves through the inspiration of the Italian educators' continual growth, to share our ongoing efforts with them, and to ask for their response. Our work with the educators of Reggio Emilia has enabled us to push as far as we have in our understanding and adaptation of the Reggio Approach and has given us the courage to continue to look ahead to where we would like to go.

With the support of Reggio Children and with Amelia's help, we have begun to host visiting days and conferences in St. Louis for educators from around the country. One of the strongest ways we can support others is through the stories of our challenges and our evolution, which continue in all aspects of our adaptation of the Reggio Approach in three different schools in St. Louis.

During the past 10 years there has been a tremendous ground swell of interest and fascination among early childhood educators in the Reggio Ap-proach. Many American educators have seen the work of the children and educa-tors of Reggio Emilia in the traveling exhibition, "The Hundred Languages of Children." Many have attended conferences, workshops, and seminars on the approach. Hundreds have participated in study tours and seminars in the Italian schools themselves, hosted by Reggio Children.

During the time of this growing interest, American educators who have studied this approach have written articles and book chapters for a variety of publications. At this point, there are three books available on the Reggio Ap-proach, all of them anthologies: *The Hundred Languages of Children*, edited by Caroline Edwards, Lella Gandini, and George Forman (1993), which includes chapters on all the fundamentals of the approach by both Italian and American educators and which is the only book which includes interviews with the late Loris Malaguzzi, the founder of the preschools in Reggio Emilia; *Reflections on the Reggio Emilia Approach*, an ERIC monograph based on papers delivered by Italian and American educators at a seminar in Reggio Emilia (Katz & Cesarone, 1994); and *First Steps Toward Teaching the Reggio Way*, edited by Joanne Hendrick (1997) and written by American educators who share their first efforts to adapt the approach in American classrooms. The work we have done in St. Louis is represented in all three of these books. This book is the first by a single author and the first to integrate the experience of a year-long internship in the preschools of Reggio Emilia, Italy, with a long-term adaptation effort in one American school.

Before I begin to tell these stories, it is important to give them a context. I will do that by briefly describing first, how my previous experience as an educator led me to want to study in the schools of Reggio Emilia; second, the historical and social context of the preschools there; third, the fundamentals of the Reggio Approach; and finally, the history behind the College School of Webster Groves in St. Louis, where I have worked for 4 years with other teachers to study and adapt the Reggio Approach.

LIFE AND WORK BEFORE REGGIO EMILIA

In 1971, I began my career as a third-grade teacher at a private school in the suburbs of Washington, DC. I quickly realized that I was most interested in children's intellectual and creative development through art media and through language. After 3 years of teaching there, I went on to study child development and arts education at Lesley College in Massachusetts and in Great Britain, where I served as an intern for a year in a school where the arts, including creative writing, were central to the curriculum. The curriculum revolved around projects and bookmaking, focusing on local resources like Georgian architecture, farm animals, and gardening.

In 1976 I found a job in Vermont as a teacher of art at the elementary level offering an opportunity to incorporate development through language and art into the classroom curriculum. I wanted children's and teachers' learning to be rooted in meaningful, connected experiences.

The highlight of this period was a collaborative project on sheep farming in Vermont with the fifth-grade social studies teacher and our students. During my favorite episode of the project, we witnessed the early spring morning birth of two lambs in a damp, dark barn. Together, we reflected on the experience, wrote poetry in the art room, and made prints and clay sculptures based on memories and sketches of the day.

After leaving classroom teaching, I worked for 6 years coordinating a Soviet–American children's art exchange and teaching arts education at the college level. In 1990, I decided to return to teaching and working directly with children. It was at this time that I heard of the preschools of Reggio Emilia. As I explain in Chapter 1, I was immediately captivated by these schools, where rich projects based on children's and teachers' explorations and discoveries unfolded. I was fascinated by the focus on language and on the multitude of arts media used by these very young children to discover and express ideas. I wanted to go there to study and learn as I had in England 15 years earlier. Through great good fortune, I was able to study alongside the Reggio Emilia educators in their schools as an intern during the academic year 1991–92.

A BRIEF HISTORY OF REGGIO EMILIA, ITALY

The town of Reggio Emilia is in the hub of a territory influenced by Etruscans and Gauls and founded by the Romans in the second century BC. During the Renaissance it was the hometown of poets Matteo Maria Boiardo and Ludovico Ariosto. Important episodes in the history of the town are the birth of the republic and the Italian national flag in 1797 and the role that the citizens of Reggio Emilia played in the movement against Nazi-Fascism, for which they received Italy's highest gold medal for military valor.

The town is located on the ancient Roman road, the Via Emilia, which crosses the entire region of Emilia Romagna from east to west. The Po River flows through the center of the region, which is bordered by the Apennine Mountains to the south and the Alps to the north. This region of 4 million inhabitants is the largest and richest region in Italy. It is rich in art and architecture, agriculture, industry, and tourism. It is also the region with the most highly developed and subsidized social services in Italy, especially in the area of child welfare (Department of Education, 1990).

The history of efforts throughout Italy to provide services and support for families and young children through private, parochial, and federal means began as early as 1820. For a short period after World War II, in 1945–46, strong local initiatives arose, especially in locations that had a tradition to support them. It was such an initiative that gave birth to the parent-run schools that were the beginnings of the Reggio Emilia preschools (Edwards, Gandini, & Forman, 1993).

In the 1950s, as educators and parents became aware of the importance of and need for early childhood education, the new ideas about progressive education of Celestin Freinet and John Dewey provoked a debate about the need to change education. In 1951, the Movement of Cooperative Education was formed, led by a strong educator named Bruno Ciari, who was appointed by the liberal administration of Bologna to direct the city school system (Edwards et al., 1993). Loris Malaguzzi was a close friend and colleague of Bruno Ciari, whose writings have become classics in Italy.

Ciari and his followers believed that "education should liberate childhood energy and capacities" (Edwards et al., 1993, p. 16) and promote the harmonious development of the whole child in communicative, social, and affective domains. Ciari encouraged educators to invite families and other citizens to participate in schools, to provide two teachers in each classroom of 20 children, to enable the staff to work collectively, and to attend carefully to the physical setting of schools.

Over the past 30 years, many different writers from different fields have contributed to the ever-evolving practice of the Reggio Approach. Among them are Urie Bronfenbrenner, Maria Montessori, Lev Vygotsky, Jean Piaget, Erik Erikson, David Hawkins, Humberto Maturana, Francisco Varela, Gregory Bateson, Howard Gardner, and Jerome Bruner.

Many regions of Italy, such as Tuscany, Lombardy, Trentino, Piedmont, Veneto, and Liguria, have established high-quality municipal early childhood systems. Emilia Romagna remains one of the most innovative, within which the town of Reggio Emilia is particularly noteworthy. The distinguishing features of the Reggio Emilia schools include the *atelier* (which is a French word meaning studio or workshop) and *atelierista* (studio teacher), the importance of the pedagogical team, the involvement and participation of elected officials in the development of the early childhood system, and a commitment to research, experimentation, communication, and documentation (Edwards et al., 1993).

Today, the municipality of Reggio Emilia supports 22 preschools and 13 infant/toddler centers. Other preschools in the city are run by the state and the Roman Catholic church. A survey in 1991 showed that 2,776 out of 2,812 3- to 6-year-old children were attending preschools. About 50% of these attended the municipal preschools. Families who wish to enroll their children apply to the municipality and are accepted on the basis of a point system. For example, single parents would receive more points because of greater need (Department of Education, 1990).

When children leave these schools at age 6, they enter a state-run, public school or a parochial school. The curriculum in these schools is prescribed by the sponsoring institution and follows a traditional model.

THE FUNDAMENTALS OF THE REGGIO APPROACH

A few short sentences cannot adequately describe the Reggio Approach. It is, nevertheless, important to include an outline of the fundamental principles that will weave themselves throughout the stories in this book. The educators in Reggio Emilia view

- *The child as protagonist.* Children are strong, rich, and capable. All children have preparedness, potential, curiosity, and interest in constructing their learning, negotiating with everything their environment brings to them. Children, teachers, and parents are considered the three central protagonists in the educational process (Gandini, 1993).
- *The child as collaborator.* Education has to focus on each child in relation to other children, the family, the teachers, and the community rather than on each child in isolation (Gandini, 1993). There is an emphasis on work in small groups. This practice is based on the social constructivist model that supports the idea that we form ourselves through our interaction with peers, adults, things in the world, and symbols (Lewin, 1995).
- *The child as communicator.* This approach fosters children's intellectual development through a systematic focus on symbolic representation, including words, movement, drawing, painting, building, sculpture, shadow play, collage, dramatic play, and music, which leads children to surprising levels of communication, symbolic skills, and creativity (Edwards et al., 1993). Children have the right to use many materials in order to discover and communicate what they know, understand, wonder about, question, feel, and imagine. In this way, they make their thinking visible through their many natural "languages." A studio teacher, trained in the visual arts, works closely with children and teachers in each school to enable children to explore many materials and to use a great number of languages to make their thinking visible.
- *The environment as third teacher.* The design and use of space encourage encounters, communication, and relationships (Gandini, 1993). There is an underlying order and beauty in the design and organization of all the space in a school and the equipment and materials within it (Lewin, 1995). Every corner of every space has an identity and a purpose, is rich in potential to engage and to communicate, and is valued and cared for by children and adults.
- *The teacher as partner, nurturer, and guide* (Edwards, 1993). Teachers facilitate children's exploration of themes, work on short- and long-term projects, and guide experiences of joint, open-ended discovery and problem solving (Edwards et al., 1993). To know how to plan and proceed with their work, teachers listen and observe children closely. Teachers ask questions; discover

children's ideas, hypotheses, and theories; and provide occasions for discovery and learning (Gandini, 1993).

- *The teacher as researcher.* Teachers work in pairs and maintain strong, collegial relationships with all other teachers and staff; they engage in continuous discussion and interpretation of their work and the work of children. These exchanges provide ongoing training and theoretical enrichment. Teachers see themselves as researchers preparing documentation of their work with children, whom they also consider researchers. The team is further supported by a *pedagogista* (pedagogical coordinator) who serves a group of schools (Gandini, 1993).

- *The documentation as communication.* Careful consideration and attention are given to the presentation of the thinking of the children and the adults who work with them. Teachers' commentary on the purposes of the study and the children's learning process, transcriptions of children's verbal language (i.e., words and dialogue), photographs of their activity, and representations of their thinking in many media are composed in carefully designed panels or books to present the process of learning in the schools. The documentation serves many purposes. It makes parents aware of their children's experience. It allows teachers to better understand children, to evaluate their own work, and to exchange ideas with other educators. Documentation also shows children that their work is valued. Finally, it creates an archive that traces the history of the school and the pleasure in the process of learning experienced by many children and their teachers (Gandini, 1993).

- *The parent as partner.* Parent participation is considered essential and takes many forms. Parents play an active part in their children's learning experience and help ensure the welfare of all the children in the school. The ideas and skills that the families bring to the school and, even more important, the exchange of ideas between parents and teachers, favor the development of a new way of educating, which helps teachers to view the participation of families not as a threat but as an intrinsic element of collegiality and as the integration of different wisdoms (Spaggiari, 1993).

THE COLLEGE SCHOOL OF WEBSTER GROVES

The brochure of the College School (1994) begins with the following statement:

> At The College School we nurture and develop the unique potential of each child through hands-on, thematic education. Our graduates leave eighth grade with a rich background in academics and the arts, and with a deep sense of who they are and what they can do. Their command of the traditional "basics"— reading, writing, and mathematics—is superior. But equally important, they become thinkers, problem solvers, and risk-takers. Above all, they have a love of learning, an excitement about life, a maturity, and a self confidence that will be the foundation for success and growth the rest of their lives. (p. 1)

The College School of Webster Groves was founded in 1963 as a laboratory school for Webster College (now Webster University). Since then, it has developed and refined the concepts and practice of experiential, integrated, thematic learning. Now a private, independent school for students from preschool through eighth grade, it remains a unique school in the St. Louis area, one that bases much of its curriculum on thematic learning and integrated approaches that cross many academic disciplines.

Adventure and environmental education are integrated into the academic curriculum, involving students, faculty, and parents in camping and expeditions, hiking and climbing, and travel to other states. Experiences in the field become one of the most important texts for children and teachers. Reflection on and analysis of these experiences in the form of writing, reading, drawing, map making, photography, and performance are part of the process of experiential learning.

Several parents and teachers and the director of the College School became very interested in the Reggio Approach through the exhibit, "The Hundred Languages of Children," which was shown in St. Louis in the fall of 1991 through the joint sponsorship of Webster University and the St. Louis Association for the Education of Young Children. They felt the approach was complementary to their own, with significant implications for their work with their very youngest students. They decided therefore to support a long-term study of the approach through a grant project.

It was at this point that the three histories I have outlined intersected. After I completed my internship in Reggio Emilia in the summer of 1992, I was hired as lead consultant for a 3-year project funded by the Danforth Foundation to study and adapt the Reggio Approach in a consortium of St. Louis schools and to develop the preschool at the College School as a reference point for study and practice.

The chapters that follow include many "mini-stories" of preschool- and kindergarten-age children, teachers, and parents who embark on journeys together. These journeys take shape in language, in drawings, in tempera paint and clay, and in the imaginations of both the children and adults. The journeys often are based on expeditions into the close-by natural world of the school yard or a neighborhood garden.

Chapters 1, 2, and 3 are based on my experience at the Diana School in Reggio Emilia in 1991–92. Chapter 1 gives an account of a day in Reggio Emilia and focuses on a school day with the 5- and 6-year-old children and their teachers at the Diana School. Chapter 2 explores the many aspects of materials and the languages of the visual arts, especially as they are used with 3-year-old children in the preschools of Reggio Emilia. Chapter 3 recounts a project on trees with 5- and 6-year-old children, which I followed during the 5 months I spent at the Diana School.

Chapters 4, 5, and 6 are based on experiences of preschool and kindergarten children and their teachers at the College School. Chapter 4 focuses on two areas: the practice of small-group conversations, and children's experiences with drawing, painting, and clay. Chapter 5 describes the transformation of the classroom environment as well as of our way of working within the space at the College School. Chapter 6 tells the story of a project on seeds, plants, and gardening that was carried out by preschool and kindergarten children and focuses on the experience and work of seven children from the class.

CHAPTER 1

The Journey

6/6/92
Reggio Emilia

It is cold today. Lacy fronds of frost weave across the window panes of my study. They sparkle and dance in a graceful pattern, fragile feathers of a frigid season. Outside, snowflakes, light and delicate, float in the breeze past the icicles glistening on the gutter, past the sturdy branches of the sweet gum tree in our neighbor's yard, past the female cardinal fluffing out her feathers against the cold. A crow calls loudly as he spreads his black wings in flight against the emerging blue, heartland sky of Missouri.

I watch memories as they float down like the softly falling snow and mingle with present thoughts. Immersing myself in memories of another year, another time and place, I look back to a year lived in Italy, where I worked in a dream of a school. I look back to live the experience again, to pull it into sharp written focus so that others might see it also. Yet this is not easy, for the experience is foreign to an American audience.

Sometimes I feel like Alice after her adventures in Wonderland or Dorothy after her journey to the Land of Oz. I lived inside a different world, inside another culture where in many ways life is perceived and lived differently than it is in this country. I lived inside schools where assumptions about who children are and what school is for are different from those held by most educators in the United States.

So, just as Lewis Carroll did with Alice and L. Frank Baum did with Dorothy, I will attempt to recreate a context for my experience in Reggio Emilia and the kind of education I witnessed there by telling a story. It will be a story about the place, the characters I met who helped me along the way, the children, the teachers, the rich and varied materials used in their learning, and one of the children's projects on trees. It also will be a story about how all these elements fit together in a continually evolving dance of connection and relationship.

HOW THE JOURNEY BEGAN

Large projected images of light-filled schools appeared on the screen. We saw children investigating the mystery of their changing shadows in the central piazza, their wonder-filled faces, glorious colors in large murals, children dancing among poppies in a huge field, the poetry of their descriptions of the color and light of the flowers, teachers' faces close to children's, also full of wonder and kindness, tablecloths at lunch, green interior gardens in the schools, many materials displayed beautifully, a project on the stone lions in the piazza unfolding through drawing and clay sculpture, music, and drama.

Then the slides stopped. A white screen remained. Students began to exit the small amphitheater classroom of the University of Vermont. The old wooden stairs creaked under them as they left. I sat stunned, full of wonder myself and full of an overwhelming certainty that I would go there, to the schools we had just seen, to live and study. I was already caught up in logistics. How would we find an apartment in Reggio Emilia? What would my husband do, and where would my sons go to school? It was May 1990.

In these slides I had seen deep connections between teachers and children. I had seen teachers support and nurture children's rich relationships with the world around them. I had seen powerful examples of the use of clay and paint, movement and measurement, drama and language to extend and deepen children's understanding of each other and the natural world. Making this kind of learning possible is my life's work.

I knew I would go there, just as I had gone to a school in England to study for a year in 1975. This was a call to continue a quest to find the kind of schools where children, teachers, and parents thrive and seem to take flight in the direction of becoming the best we can all become through challenging our minds, engaging our hearts, using our hands, and honoring each other and the world in all its complex beauty and mystery. It was a call to journey out of the American mind, beyond the limits of logic, the constraints of the norm, the dullness of the known, the doom of boredom, the trap of the predictable.

I am in love with the Italian culture. I traveled there for the first time when I was 15 with my mother and sister. I love the land, the ancient history, the richly woven culture, the flamboyance of the Italian personality, the language. I began to study the language seriously in 1989 after my fourth trip there. I was becoming fluent.

After living in England in 1975–76, and after watching my brother's children become fluent in French and change their world view through living in France, I had dreamed of living abroad with my young family. All the pieces of the puzzle began to fit together. We were all ready for a change. I took the lead.

I attended several conferences and met Carlina Rinaldi and Vea Vecchi, both of whom would become my mentors in Italy. I wrote an official letter of request asking to be accepted as an intern for a year. I applied for a small American travel fellowship, which I received. I visited the schools for the first time in May 1991. My request was granted. My husband Ashley, my sons Alden, age 11, and Christopher, age 8, and I arrived in Reggio Emilia at the end of August 1991.

With Carlina Rinaldi's help, we found a third-floor apartment in an eight-story building on the edge of the old walled town. It was one of the first buildings to be built after the war, mostly of concrete. Sound traveled right through the walls so we heard everyone's television, especially Signora Parker's, our neighbor, who was 92 and very deaf. The apartment was sparsely furnished, but spacious and adequate for us. It was not at all what we had in mind. But slowly, we all began to get used to it. French doors opened out to a small balcony overlooking the piazza below. To the right we could see the public gardens, across a major busy street. We were in a convenient location, a short distance from the Diana School, to which I walked or rode my bike for the first 5 months of my internship.

A MORNING IN REGGIO EMILIA

I sit on our balcony and watch the early morning activity begin. This morning the piazza is cool. There is a darkening bank of gray clouds to the southwest. There is only a breeze after yesterday's strong wind. I hear the loud flapping of pigeon wings as a group of birds takes off. I hear the screech and clanking of a heavy shutter open below, probably Teresa, the fruit and vegetable lady. The mourning doves coo their guttural calls. A distant train rumbles as it approaches the station, and the high train whistle sounds. The first bus thunders by. I see the swallows for miles. They are everywhere. They swoop and sail on the air currents. Two people walk slowly across the piazza to the Forno, the bakery, which has just opened.

The building across from us, which is the color of tomato soup, is brilliantly lit by the angle of the morning sun. The windows are like so many eyes, the shutters like eyelids, as they open to let their inhabitants survey the day. My gaze travels across the geraniums on Signora Parker's balcony, past the flags of the Astoria Hotel to the public gardens, then over the tiled patches of roofs which fit together like puzzle pieces, and finally to the two towers of the church of San Francesco, which rise beyond the roof tops. The bells of San Francesco and the duomo in the town center begin to peal. Deep, sonorous tones, each bell a different pitch, a different cadence, like a waterfall of ancient sounds, they call out the hours, just as they have for centuries.

The rest of the family begins to stir. Alden and Chris dress and come into the kitchen for breakfast—the Italian version of Kellogg's Corn Flakes, yet slightly less substantial and quicker to become soggy in milk from a box. Fresh milk is very hard to come by here, and children seem to drink water.

They pack up their carefully done homework—answers to math problems written out in sentences and small compositions written in a cursive they are both trying hard to improve because their classmates' handwriting is so impressive. Alden takes on learning the language with a vengeance and quickly begins communicating in sentences. Christopher is baffled and remains silent for weeks, which is unusual for him.

The boys attend one of the two schools in the city that employ a teacher who works with non-Italian-speaking children to help them learn the language. Like most Italian children, they attend a state elementary school, which follows a prescribed and demanding curriculum determined by the Ministry of Education in Rome. First-grade children learn upper- and lowercase print and cursive writing before the first semester is over. In this town, where there are hardly ever any tourists except those visiting the now renowned preschools, American children are a rare phenomenon. Alden and Chris are well-liked because they are from such a famous and unknown place as the United States.

At 8:00 they head out the heavy metal door, down the cavernous staircase, and out to unlock their rickety second-hand bikes, which have been generously loaned to us for the year. Riding to school takes 10 minutes through the maze of old streets and piazzas that make up the center of town. It is easy to become disoriented and lost in dead ends or wrong turns.

Once, early in the year, Christopher went out to ride to a friend's house and didn't come home until almost dark. He explained that he had become lost riding in circles in unfamiliar territory. Finally, he came out at his school and he knew how to get home from there.

After the boys leave, Ashley and I often decide to go down to The Lady Bar for morning coffee. The cafe is owned by two sisters, Marisa and Mirella. They are glad to see us because we are a friendly anomaly to them, too. They like to help us with the language, ask us over and over again how we could ever have left home, and tell us that Italians aren't like that, that they would never think of leaving home with the whole family for a whole year.

This cafe and others are called bars because people often stand up to drink their coffee, or beer or aperitif served later in the day. It is a place to sip a quick demitasse espresso or, if there are tables, to sit and read the paper or discuss politics or family matters with friends and neighbors. The bar here is a dark green marble. There are clean, white crocheted doilies under a copper sugar bowl and under a vase of fresh freesias. A spotlight highlights the opening buds, which tremble slightly under the breeze from the overhead fan. A case of fresh pastries is reflected in the mirror across the small room.

The coffee is rich, deep, dark, and serious. For coffee lovers, it has an intoxicating aroma. We ask for "due cappuccini" served in thick white china cups. The sound of the heavy lira pieces on the marble is punctuated by the sound of the china collecting in the sink. This morning coffee is an Italian ritual. We feel lucky to be able to partake of it not as tourists, but as foreigners who are trying to settle in and understand and appreciate the culture and the people more deeply.

What we understand is that every detail in this bar is important. It is welcoming and beautiful and cared for like a home. It is managed by two sisters who serve regular customers like guests. It is a delight to the senses and to the soul. Even though we do not stay long, it is a lovely way to begin the day.

Ashley returns to the apartment to continue work on a house he is designing for friends in Vermont. I unlock my bicycle and ride around the apartment building out into Piazza Vallisneri. Teresa is already helping customers select potatoes and carrots for today's minestrone. We wave to one another. I also wave to Francesco, the barber, who has taken a special liking to my son, Chris.

I cross the street and the Astoria Hotel parking lot and enter the public gardens through a small opening in the hedge that borders the Astoria property. I ride to the right so I can approach the Diana school the long way in order to have more time in the midst of the trees. We, who are accustomed to being surrounded by trees in Vermont, find it strange to live in this old city with so little green. I relish my time to glide under the sweet gums and sycamores, and to marvel at the huge, majestic cypress. This park, or public gardens as they are called, isn't very big, maybe 15 acres. The grass grows wild and is mowed only once every 2 months. There are wide paths covered with small stones for children to ride their bikes on and for adults to promenade. Near the center of the park there is a double-tiered round fountain, surrounded by three cupid figures. The bottom of the fountain is covered with mosses and algae and has become completely green. Near the fountain are two outdoor cafes, which are open only during the warm months.

On the opposite edge of the public gardens, nestled under the tall trees, lies the Diana School (see Figure 1.1). My very first trip here, the first time I set foot out of the hotel, I walked directly to the school without knowing where it was or where I was going. It was Sunday. I peered in through a gate and saw myself reflected in a mirror, which had been placed over a single brick.

THE DIANA SCHOOL

Every morning around 8:30, I arrive along with children and parents, some on foot, some by bicycle. Children ride on seats in front of the handlebars in Italy, leading the way, free to see up, down, and 180 degrees around them. Entering

FIGURE 1.1.   The Diana School Viewed from the Public Gardens

through the big gate, I lean my old, rickety, thick-tired bike against the outside kitchen wall of the school next to a beautiful, new, white bike that belongs to Ida, one of the cooks.

I love to walk in the front doors of the school every morning. It is a familiar and delicious routine to step into the entry way greeted by photographs of all the teachers, and out into the central atrium or piazza. The space is breathtakingly beautiful, with a vaulting ceiling, an interior garden court to each side viewed through glass walls, and the *atelier* ahead vibrant with color and reflected glass. Beyond the *atelier*, one sees the branches of the cypress through glass walls. The trees left behind in the public gardens greet you again the minute you enter the school. It is a jewel of a school, catching the sun and reflecting the light, sparkling with color and transparency, busy with the beginnings of the morning (see Plate 1).

I greet the cooks—Ida, Antonella, and Nadia—in the kitchen to the left as I hang up my coat. The kitchen is warm and bright. Fresh fruit snacks are being prepared for the children—sliced and peeled apples, juicy pears, or small bunches of grapes in glass bowls. Children arrive in the kitchen from each class in pairs to pick up the fruit and to tell the cooks how many will be eating lunch at school that day. Lunch for teachers and children is in preparation. The sharp smell of garlic, the fragrance of pungent tomato sauces and simmering vegetables fills the room. The sunlight filters through the gauzy curtains and plays on the shining stainless steel sink and island stove. A yellow and white checkered tablecloth covers the long rectangular table where the teachers and the cooks will eat lunch together later in the day. The kitchen is immaculately clean and beautifully equipped with mixers and bowls, an espresso machine, wide wooden counter tops, white china. It is like the most welcoming of homes.

In the central atrium, or piazza as it is called, I greet children who are already dressing up in fanciful clothes inside a curved structure with hooks hung inside at the children's level. Benedetta, a 3-year-old, wears a skirt as a head-dress. Ilaria is fully dressed in a long skirt and flowered hat pulled down to shade one eye. They may stay in these clothes all day. On the other side of the room, Michele and Sara lie on their backs watching themselves multiply into infinity inside a wooden triangle mirrored on all three interior sides.

From here, through the layers of glass, I can see the bent heads of Vea Vecchi, the *atelierista*, and Marina Mori, one of the two teachers of the 5-year-olds this year, talking together in the *atelier*. They are deciding what to discuss next with the group of 5-year-old boys who have been drawing trees changing through the seasons.

The *atelier* has a high ceiling with glass to the peak on two sides, allowing one to look out on the busy piazza room on one side and to the trees on the other. The cypress and Norwegian spruce trees tower above the school. Their branches brush the roof. On foggy days, the school is shrouded in gray mist and seems to be protected by these guardian trees.

The room is full of natural objects that delight the eye—there are pink and white seashells, smooth stones, and pieces of gnarled wood displayed in pleasing patterns on a shelf near the door. A large, robust philodendron sends variegated green and white leaves cascading down from the rafters where it is perched. The kiln is on today, firing clay lizards and snails and vessels draped with clay leaves, which have been appearing around a round, flat basket on the large square table in the middle of the room.

In the back of the *atelier* there are shelves and open racks of children's paintings, collages of natural materials, photographs, and typewritten documents. Near the back windows there is a large space for working on murals on the floor. One such mural hangs on a back wall. It is a summertime painting, tempera on paper, full of lavenders, peaches, and deep reds. Silver and white spirals of waves roll toward a triple-stacked raspberry and lime ice cream cone, a house painted in pastels, and a tropical bird. A hot red sun with undulating yellow rays fills the whole space of the *atelier* with warmth. This is a dream painting—a dream of summer. It reminds me of Chagall.

I put my briefcase on the small wicker couch in the back corner of the *atelier* as I do every morning, take out my notebook, and walk over to begin to listen to Vea and Marina. I have been following the work of the four 5-year-old boys they are discussing, and I am curious to hear the morning's ideas.

Both of them are animated, moving their hands, pointing out features of the drawings. Vea asks Marina about particulars of the boys' most recent conversation to try to understand how their ideas are evolving.

These two women are wonderful to watch. Their way of communicating is like a dance. They have worked as partners for 15 years, and they know each other well, yet the material is fresh, always fresh. They are on their toes, their minds are alive, their experience with this way of working runs deep. They are working with ideas, children's ideas represented in graphics—soft pencils, colored pencils, and colored markers. They have invited and challenged the boys to represent several of their theories about trees through drawing. They have asked them to work together, to pool their ideas, their individual styles of working and particular strengths. This is, of course, the way Vea and Marina are working now—in concert, in harmony, in depth, in collaboration.

Vea is in her 50s. She came to work originally with Loris Malaguzzi when she was very young, having graduated from the Italian equivalent of art school. She has shoulder-length, soft red hair, which curls around her face like a lion's mane. She is dressed in short, gray, flannel shorts, tights, and a soft gray sweater that comes to her waist, and heavy, thick-soled, black tie shoes that she wears with everything. She is practical but elegant. She moves with a graceful, swaying gait. She speaks with her slender fingers. Her green eyes glitter with fiery intensity and soft humor at the same time. She is an orchestrator and a directress. She has an aura that is commanding, a sense of delight, and a laugh that cascades. She is alive, fully in the moment, on the edge of learning and new ideas. When she gives slide presentations she uses slides from yesterday's work, with ideas for tomorrow. She weaves ideas of a life's work skillfully with passion and poetry. She can be demanding, difficult, single-minded, tough with everyone. She is a mentor. I am privileged to work in her space.

Marina Mori is my soulmate, my first Italian friend. I felt a connection with her right away. Her son, Andrea, is my son Christopher's age. She is warm. All in auburn today, with hair falling down her back, bright hazel eyes, nut-brown corduroy shorts, earth-toned patterned sweater. I am able to work in her room with the 5-year-olds and the tree project. For me, it seems that the center of the world is this school, this classroom, this project. Sometimes it almost takes my breath away. How could I be so lucky as to live in this country that I love, with my family, a short walk from this dream school where I can work every day with Vea as a mentor and Marina, a dear friend, alongside the oldest children in the school, who are discovering and getting to know the trees.

Now, I follow Marina and Vea's conversation, their exchange of ideas, their excitement, their wondering together, as I have followed many similar early morning discussions with Vea and Marina and other teachers. This way of touching base, discussing what has happened with children, trying to understand, agreeing what might be discussed with the children next, what materials to suggest, how to follow the process of their learning, is part of the daily routine at the Diana School. It happens with Vea and at least one of the pairs of teachers from all three classes in the morning before the day begins and again in the late morning as the children are finishing their morning work. At the end of the morning, the *atelier* often is bustling with teachers showing each other what amazing things happened that morning, what ideas children have had and how they have represented the ideas in words, gestures, drawing, clay, paint, light, shadows, wire.

The teachers in the preschools of Reggio Emilia have learned to work in this way under the guidance of educational philosopher and principal founder of the movement behind these schools, Loris Malaguzzi. Among others, Vea Vecchi and Carlina Rinaldi worked alongside Malaguzzi for over 20 years to help him build the principles behind the approach and the strong practice that is based on them.

The *atelieristi* receive training in a preuniversity level art school, and the classroom teachers are trained in a vocational school of education. This is also at the preuniversity level. Neither receive training in the Reggio Approach before they arrive at the schools. They are trained through working closely with more experienced teachers and through seminars conducted throughout the year by the *pedagogisti*, teachers, and *atelieristi*.

This morning, after Marina and Vea finish their exchange, Marina and I walk together into her classroom. There are three classrooms in all, each with 25 children and two team teachers. The children from this class, *i grandi* (the big ones), as they are called, are engaged in greeting each other, hanging up their jackets, playing games, talking in groups in the piazza room, adding to an ongoing block construction in the corner, or perhaps responding to a message found in their mailbox. Paola, Marina's co-teacher, is greeting parents and children. There is a busy, purposeful feeling throughout the school.

The first detail that always catches my eye when I enter this room is an ever-changing display of clay figures and creatures made by children, on a shelf that defines the entryway to the room. Today, several families of clay ants crawling on small wooden logs, and a pair of red clay spiders are reflected in a mirror that rests on the top of the shelf. A vase of autumn asters from a teacher's or child's country weekend walk reflects delicate lavender blooms in a small standing mirror at the end of the shelf near the door.

The main room is spacious and airy because of high ceilings and low windows along one entire wall. A housekeeping area lined with mirrors is located behind a shelf in one corner. A block area, including many different types of provocative materials such as tubes, cones, hoops, swags of fabric, shells and stones, and wooden animals and people, fills an area on the opposite side of the room between an ample three-staired set of risers and the windowed wall. Individual boxes for messages hang above the risers next to a writing area with a computer and printer. There are three rectangular yellow tables with small chairs in the center of the room, and one larger white adult-sized table and chairs, which also are used by children, at the end of the room next to the windows.

On the walls there are enticing photographs of a group of children standing in the shadows of the huge sycamore tree outside the school, and close-up shots of their hands moving over the bark and of their captivated faces in the midst of buds beginning to open in the spring. Alongside the large photographs, there are intricate, detailed line drawings of leaves, in multiple shades of green fine-lined marker; tempera paintings of layered bark and the concentric circles of a cross-section of a tree trunk in rich browns, greens, and blacks; pencil drawings of buds and blossoms; and children's ideas about these phenomena typewritten underneath, such as, "The buds are delicate and light green because they are just born and they are still in a cradle."

At around 9:00, after the parents have gone, Marina and Paola call the group together for a meeting. The children gather on the wooden risers as the pears, which were prepared earlier in the kitchen, are served. Marina begins, "Well, how was your weekend? Who picked those beautiful flowers? Where were you? Carla, you were away for 3 days. Tell us about your trip to the mountains. What did you find? What did you bring back?"

Children and teachers chat, catch up, and share the pleasure of each other's company. There isn't any rush, there isn't a feeling that there is a need for control on the teachers' part. It is just a pleasure. "Well, what do we have going today?" Paola takes the lead.

> Carla, you, Agnese, and Elise were working on the class newspaper you had organized. Would you like to continue? Would you like to work on the computer today? Some children have been invited to help the 3-year-olds with working with wire. Who would like to do that? Are there two of you who would like to play checkers? Two can continue to use the colored inks at the light table to paint your plants you brought back after the summer. Bobo, Marco, Ale, and Omar, you are still working on your drawings of your theories about trees with Marina in the mini-*atelier*, aren't you? Are there other ideas you would like to suggest?

As the morning's work begins, I follow Marina and the group of boys into the mini-*atelier*, a small room attached to the main classroom. The quartet of 5-year-old boys and Marina begin to spread out their tree drawings on the table. The room has two glass walls with doors, like the larger *atelier*. One side faces the classroom and the other opens out to the trees and shrubs in the back of the school and the public gardens. The square table in the middle of the room is just big enough for eight child-sized chairs. There are deep, open shelves on one wall that hold many varieties and sizes of paper. The top of the shelf displays clay animals and heads sculpted by children; open jars of beads, seeds, and buttons; and transparent boxes of small shiny papers, tissue papers, twines, and ribbons. On the opposite wall a tall gray metal shelf stores pencils of all kinds, pens, and markers; watercolors and inks; brushes and clay tools; varieties of wire and wire cutters.

Francesca and Claudia, who have chosen to paint at the light table, collect the inks and brushes they need in the mini-*atelier* and continue past us to another small adjacent room that houses a collection of musical instruments, cassette tapes of music from all over the world, and a tape recorder. This small room is also the home of the light table, a rectangular table with a semitransparent, plastic top and a fluorescent light mounted underneath that can be switched on and off. This table glows with warmth and radiant light through inks and watercolors, tissue papers, and colored acetates. Usually used by architects and designers, this versatile piece of equipment has been brought into the schools to offer children and teachers another possibility for looking at the world from another perspective, one filled with light.

The two girls choose a cassette of Peruvian flute music and begin to organize themselves to paint. Two healthy green plants with pink spotted leaves spill over their pots placed on the back of the light table. Francesca gently examines the leaves of her plant. Claudia begins to paint stems with vibrant greens and pinks.

All of these 5- and 6-year-old children are fully engaged in their work from shortly after 9 until sometime after 11. At this time, some children finish the morning's work and wander out the doors of their classroom to play outside under their trees, in the wooden tree house climber, on the merry-go-round. The young waiters and waitresses whose turn it is to set the tables return 15 minutes before lunch at noon. The pair of children begin with the tablecloths, then the silverware and glasses, finally arranging each child's cloth napkin, brought from home, at his or her place.

At noon the tempting smells of the *primo piato* (the first course) bring the children in to wash their hands and sit in anticipation of their midday meal. Today it is pasta served in heavy, wide-rimmed low bowls, fat chunks of parmesan cheese, and pieces of erbazzone, a local thin-crusted spinach torte. Lunch, or "pranzo," is such a pleasure for them. They have learned from their families to enjoy the time together, to savor the food, to take their time. One teacher from each pair helps serve and supervise the meal, while the other sets up the cots in the classroom for nap time.

After lunch, the curtains are pulled, and the room is darkened while the children settle down for their rest time. Today Paola reads them the story of Hanzel and Gretel from a large collection of fairy tales. Soon most of these children have fallen asleep.

Now it is time for the teachers' lunch. This time of the day is a treat for me for many reasons. The contrast to the American habit of gulping down a sandwich or a cafeteria school lunch is obvious. The civilized, gracious manner in which the food is prepared, served, and enjoyed is an education for me. The range, depth, and engagement in our daily conversation are a delight. Pressing conversations of an organizational nature about work do not come up. If the conversation turns to work in the school, it takes on a philosophical, pedagogical twist, as if viewed from a wide-angle lens. Often, teachers' families, politics, friends, or shared memories are topics. There is always immense enjoyment in each other's company as a staff, including the cooks. In other words, business is not the subject. An Italian friend once explained to me, "We do not have working lunches with agendas in Italy. They give us indigestion and do not respect the work or the meal or the time together."

Today, after pranzo, Marina and Vea talk again about the trees the boys have drawn. We enter the room of the 5- and 6-year-olds quietly, as the children are still sleeping, and pass through to the mini-*atelier* where Paola has been transcribing the conversation that took place that morning. In low voices Marina describes what happened with the four boys, and Vea gives her opinion: "They have accepted the challenge to represent the trees through the seasons according to their theories. Now they realize that all their drawings are of different trees. Can you decide together to choose one of their trees to use for a base for each season? I think they could come to that conclusion." The conversation continues as they search to understand the children's ideas and how to proceed.

The children slowly wake up and are greeted by a snack prepared by the cooks and auxiliary helpers. It is 4:00 and many parents or grandparents arrive to take children home. Others stay until 5:00 or 6:00 for an after-school program.

I prepare to go home as well. It has been a full day, and I am ready for a bike ride through the countryside with my boys and Ashley. I collect my things and say good-bye for the day. I wheel my bicycle through the big double gate and out into the park. I wind my way home past park benches filled with amorous teenage couples, past old men talking in clusters, past mothers and small children playing on the swings, past stone statues, and under the canopy of sweet gum leaves gradually turning yellow under the October sun. Again, I think about how lucky I am to have been given the privilege to live and study in Reggio Emilia, Italy.

Later that evening, after our bike ride past vineyards and barnyards and fields of poplars, we are treated to a delicious pasta meal made in our kitchen by our new friends, Amelia Gambetti, her husband Sergio, Giovanni Piazza, and our neighbor and adopted aunt, Carlina Rinaldi. Amelia is a teacher, and Giovanni, the *atelierista* at La Villetta School, where I will serve as an intern later that spring. Carlina is the director of all the *pedagogisti* for all the preschools and infant/toddler centers.

These wonderful friends have taken us under their wing. They want to make sure that we feel at home and that we learn the proper way to cook pasta and make simple sauces. Amelia takes over our kitchen, laughing, as she chops the garlic for the *sugo al pomodoro*. Later, as we devour Amelia's pasta, they all enjoy practicing their English and marvel at the novelty of a whole American family that has made its way to their small Italian city, all for the purpose of studying their way of educating young children.

Plate 1. The piazza of the Diana School

Plate 2. "The trees are important because they are beautiful"

Plate 3. The preschool *atelier* at the College School

Plate 4. The garden mural

Plate 5. Kateri's grow table design

Plate 6. Milla's second grow table design

Plate 7. Adam's bean portrait

CHAPTER 2

The Pleasure and Power of Playing with Materials

6/18/95
River
Sculpture

For as long as I can remember I have loved paints, pens, clay, beautiful paper of various weights and textures, richly patterned fabrics, thick yarns and light-weight embroidery threads of rainbow colors and earth tones. At the same time, I have always felt an affinity for the small objects of the natural world that I could pick up and take home—smooth, round stones, nubby brown pinecones of all shapes and sizes, pink, luminescent shells left on the wet sand of a sloping beach as the waves recede, swirling autumn leaves falling and settling at my feet.

The pigments of paint, the textures of yarns, the weight and wetness of clay come from the earth. They are the earth. We often use these materials to make connections, to build bridges, to create our own renderings and responses to what we experience in the world. We play with them as we play with stones or shells on the beach to create our own arrangements, to make our own beauty, to reach out to the natural world and participate in it.

If we learn to love words—the sound of them, the feel of them in our mouths, the many meanings and mysteries they hold, the way they can make metaphors, weave tales, tell secrets, we use them in much the same way we use these materials of the earth—to make connections with the world and with each other, to make a context for ourselves.

We do not do this in isolation. We do it most often in the company of friends or for a wider audience. We invite response to what we do, whether we do it alone, in pairs, or in a group. We want to know if what we make, what we say, what we write, what we shape, makes sense, communicates, tells the story we had in mind.

Recently, my family and I attended a retreat at a camp in Virginia. Thirty adults and children came together for 4 days of quiet contemplation, heartfelt exchange, joyful play, and mindful community making.

There were no phones, TVs, VCRs, video games, computers, cars, mov-ies, malls, or other twentieth-century distractions. What a pleasure to see chil-dren from 5 to 15 and adults alongside them awaken to the natural world, play in it, and respond to it. Wild flowers and grasses were arranged on the tables, wild berries appeared in muffins baked by children, brown pebbles lined up on the railing of the porch in ever-changing configurations, watercolor paintings and mandala drawings hung on the log walls of our dining hall.

One day, in the river that ran through the camp land, statues of stones, stacked from large to small in perfect balance, began to take shape across a shallow, stony part of the river. The statues were made first by a father, then by the teenagers, and were added to later by other adults and small children. They still stand as a tribute to our time together beside the gurgling river. The vertical stones carefully placed in a complete composition were our river version of the Ryoanji Zen garden in Kyoto, Japan. They are a response to the river, a game of stones, a game of balance, a game of the generations. They are an elegant counterpoint to flowing water and riverbed stones heretofore destined to lie forever underwater, mastered by the river. This building with natural materials, in response to a natural setting, and playful yet serious collaboration between children and adults reminds me of my experience in the Reggio Emilia pre-schools.

There are many remarkable things about the municipal preschools of Reggio Emilia, Italy. What seems most remarkable to me, however, is the educators' deep understanding of the power of materials and of words to shape experience. Alongside this is a respect for the complexity and beauty of the natural world, and for the intelligence and creativity of young children and the adults who work with them. In this chapter, I will describe the variety and beauty of the materials that are offered to children in the preschools of Reggio Emilia. I will then tell a series of stories about how teachers present these materials to children, how children make use of them, and how teachers interpret what children do with them.

MATERIALS IN THE REGGIO EMILIA PRESCHOOLS

The wealth of materials that are available to the children in the preschools of Reggio Emilia is staggering. By this I do not mean wealth as in cost, though good quality materials are purchased by the schools. Rather, the wealth is in the variety of materials available to the children, and in ingenious ideas for their use. There is also a wealth of time given by the teachers to preparation and presentation of the materials and to thoughtful reflection on how and what the children make.

What do you find in the way of materials if you explore one of the preschools in Reggio Emilia? You find freshly mixed tempera paint in many shades and tints in clear glass jars; big brushes, little brushes, flat and round brushes, paper of all colors and sizes, including many varieties of transparent and semitransparent clear and colored paper. You discover clay in many contexts and often in relation to other materials like wood, cardboard, wire, small bits of mirrors, colored glass, or shells (see Figure 2.1). Another "media" can be uncovered in what are referred to in the Reggio Emilia preschools as natural materials and colors: leaves, seeds, cones, twigs, dried flower petals, and even different colored earth and sand. These natural materials are used to "paint" with and/or are arranged in collages (see Figure 2.2).

Good-quality markers and colored pens of all colors and nibs, soft and hard pencils, soft, oil pastel crayons, and colored inks are arranged and accessible on open shelves. There are also many different types of wire, small pieces of wire mesh, shiny pieces of paper, and small, child-sized wire cutters carefully stored in open bins. On other shelves, boxes of all types of ribbons, yarns, twine, embroidery floss, and threads, and looms made of cardboard, wood, twigs, and wire are ready for use at any time. Light is considered another material. Through working directly on transparent paper placed on a light table, children can play with the effects of layering colored tissue, drawing with markers or colored inks, or arranging collage materials surrounded and immersed in light.

Looking further, you will notice ever-evolving collections of collage materials like buttons, colorful candy wrappers, sequins, small shapes of cut paper of all varieties, found objects, small photocopies of individual black and white photographs of the children, small and large magazine photographs, photocopies of words or words from magazines, photocopies of children's names, and cardboard of all shapes and types (see Figure 2.3).

All these materials are beautifully organized and maintained by adults and

FIGURE 2.1. An Example of a Child's Exploration of Clay

children together. Most materials are housed in the *atelier*, which is located in a central place in the school, or the mini-*ateliers*, which are located adjacent to each of the three classrooms.

The children begin to work with most of these materials at the age of 3. In fact, if the children attend a *nido* (translated as nest), for children ages 3 months to 3 years, they have a chance to use many of the materials as toddlers. The different materials are available to children in much the same way blocks and the dress-up corner are available—as a choice for a small group of children during the morning work time of approximately 2 hours. The materials are offered in many different ways, sometimes with specific proposals and suggestions and sometimes without. Often, simply the way the materials are presented suggests a starting point without any words spoken. Sometimes the materials become part of a project that can extend for a week, several weeks, or several months.

In the beginning, the children primarily explore and play with the materials, learning the qualities of each one as well as the possibilities and limits of each through their experience. They often play, imagine, and invent stories through imaginative play using the materials in the same way they do blocks and dress-ups.

What follows are several brief sketches of very young children's exploration and play, primarily using clay. The examples come from observations and

FIGURE 2.2. A Collection of Natural Materials

later discussions with teachers at both La Villetta and the Diana School. The teachers are Giovanni Piazza, *atelierista*, and Paola Barchi, then teacher of the 3-year-old children, both from La Villetta, and Laura Rubizzi, then teacher of the 3-year-old children at the Diana School.

Animal Dens

A group of 3-year-olds and their teacher at La Villetta take an autumn walk in the big field in back of their school. They discover holes and tunnels made by small animals. Back in the classroom, with the help of their teacher, Paola, they remember what they saw, smelled, felt, and discovered. Their conversation is recorded and transcribed and later displayed with some of their other work.

Over the next few days, they have the chance to use several materials to help them remember, explore, recreate, and invent their own animal dens. One day, a group of three children work with soft oil crayons of greens, yellows, oranges, and browns on 8 × 11 inch white paper in the mini-*atelier*. They experiment with different ways to use the crayons. They use strokes that resemble grass in the wind, or layer greens and yellows, like matted grasses, mix colors, and make dark patches nestled in between other marks.

FIGURE 2.3.   Materials for Making Messages

They explain what they have made to their teacher. She writes their words on a piece of acetate, over the parts of the picture they refer to. The oil pastels of the fields and dens are displayed with the acetate directly on top, so you can read the words of the children and find the reference points below. You also can lift the acetate up to see the drawing without the superimposed words. Another day, a different small group of children will have a chance to remember and represent their experience in materials and words.

In the *atelier* a small group of four children work with Giovanni inventing and recreating animal dens with clay. Each has his or her own soccer ball-sized piece of clay. There is a box of small plastic animals in the middle of the table. Giovanni tells the children that he knows they have been discovering animal dens outside and talking about them in their class. He asks the children if they would like to use the clay and maybe the animals to make their own dens.

The children, who have discussed these possibilities earlier with their teachers and Giovanni, begin to dig holes, hide animals, make up stories about wolves and foxes, moles and mice, predators and prey. They relive their discoveries, weave their new ideas and inventions into their previous experience, enjoy the fantasy and the reality of the stories and creations they make together. The clay is a vehicle for all of this. As they work and play, they are learning the language of clay.

Spaceships

In the classroom of the 3-year-olds at the Diana School, three children start work with individual large blocks of clay. There are rectangular pieces of stiff wire netting available if the children want to use them. There is no specific proposal. One child begins with the idea of a spaceship; another, a person on a motorcycle. They manipulate the clay, form long coils of clay and connect them, add and subtract clay, add pieces of wire. The boy with the motorcycle is attracted to the spaceship and decides to transform his clay piece into a spaceship too.

Laura, one of their teachers, observes and takes written and graphic notes about what is happening. That is, what the boys say as they work, how they work, and what they actually do with the clay. She decides with them to find some plastic straws in addition to the other materials because she senses that they would like to make more physical connections between the two ships. A new collaborative invention in spaceship conflict and cooperation begins. The clay, the wire, and then the straws enable the children to invent and develop a story, to transform the clay and the story many times in the course of the morning, and to build a relationship between the two of them through their collaboration.

At the end of the morning, in all the cases with clay mentioned above, the clay was put back in the bin to be used another day, like the blocks and dress-ups, to make new inventions and stories.

"The Hundred Languages of Children"

As with the clay, the children have many opportunities to experiment with, play with, and develop knowledge and competence in the languages of all the other materials mentioned previously: tempera paint, watercolor, wire, weaving, collage, natural materials, cardboard/paper construction, and light, color, and transparency at the light table. These media, alongside words, music, movement, dramatic play, numbers, block construction, and shadow play, are among what the educators in Reggio Emilia have called "the hundred languages of children" (Edwards et al., 1993).

These materials have the power to engage children's minds, bodies, and emotions. Their evocative power calls the children into the processes of weaving what they have already experienced in the world with their new perceptions and sensibilities. In this way, the children continue to build and rebuild, through the materials, an ever-expanding awareness and understanding of the world and their place in it. Each material offers its own particular qualities to the child. Each child offers his or her particular qualities to each material. Each new material gives the child a chance to build another kind of understanding of the richness and complexity of the world.

VEA'S STORIES

Vea Vecchi, the *atelierista* at the Diana School, became my mentor. Because she was busy following and documenting the projects and developments in all three classrooms at the Diana School and in giving presentations in Italy and abroad, she was not always available. However, she helped me whenever she could with questions I had about the nature of the work as it unfolded with children and teachers at the Diana School.

I also learned from her through listening to many formal and informal meetings between Vea and the teachers, and through careful observation, documentation, and participation with teachers and children in the classroom and the *atelier*. I loved to listen to Vea's vivid descriptions of the work of children and teachers when she made slide presentations. I was fortunate to attend a series of lectures that she gave to teachers of infants and toddlers in Modena, Italy in January 1992.

It was through listening to these presentations and through informal interviews that I began to recognize the following themes in all her work with children—the cultivation of a sense of wonder and amazement, the invitation to notice and to play with everyday phenomena that often go unnoticed, the encouragement to make connections between lived experience and materials, in order to shape, communicate, and hold the experience rather than letting it disperse and lose significance. Finally, I began to understand the delicate role of the adult in allowing the child to take the lead while also encouraging the child to wonder, notice, and make the relationships that would allow a new level of understanding to develop.

To provide an inside glimpse into the way the educators in the Reggio Emilia preschools think about and use materials with children, I will now retell some of Vea's stories about her work with 3-year-olds. Because of my focus on the natural world, the following stories have nature and natural phenomena as their main focus. They come from informal interviews I had with Vea and from the presentations I attended. With her permission, these are told in her words, as I have transcribed and translated them.

The Sky

In this story Vea gives an example of a way she accompanies young children as they make connections between a material like tempera paint and their experience in the natural world.

> The children often paint independently, with many gradations of color. Every once in a while, we can throw them some provocations to enliven their work and to avoid the risks of excessive repetition. We can create situations that permit the children to make unusual connections. One day, I put a Plexiglas mirror out on the ground outside so that we could walk on the mirror. It became a great provocation. We walked on the sky and in some way, we were able to touch it.
>
> Inside the classroom, we projected pieces of blue acetate onto the walls with an overhead projector, simulating the colors of the sky. Then a cloud arrived. We blew it out of the window. Then we played a game with slides. You can play this game with slides of the sky, the sea, or the desert. I think it is important that the children enter into this "theater of virtual reality" so that they can move in a different way according to the provocations that you give.

In this case, we know there are many conditions of the sky and many "faces" of the clouds. You need to play on and with the differences, the modifications, even when the children are very young. We projected slides of a storm, the sunset, the sunrise, and the sky seen from above as from an airplane. The children walked on the clouds and "flew" with their arms as they pretended to be angels and airplanes. Everyone participated. These are beautiful games. These are games that excite children's interest.

Then, we put a big, transparent plastic sheet on the window and they painted the sky, the clouds, whatever they wanted to paint. And you see, some remembered the sunset; maybe they wanted to use red. Another remembered the storm and wanted to use gray. Some remembered, some didn't. However, the games they played with the slides and this painting are filled with significance. In this case, we could say that these children have made a first collective work born of a common experience. What they have done together gives an imprint of identity both to themselves and to their own marks.

Earth

In the following three stories, Vea gives some examples of ways she has explored the natural world and used natural materials with 3-year-old children.

Discovering Color, Texture, and Light

The discovery and exploration of the out-of-doors shouldn't be done in a hurry. We need to give children enough time—a long time—to feel the tactility, hear the sounds, smell the smells. These sensory images are like pages of a book that they put inside themselves. They are "informers and elaborators" of the memory. The stronger the images are, the more they remain in the memory and the more children can "narrate" them (with the voice, with music, with dance, with drawing, with painting . . .) when they are back in school. It is clear that children live these explorations in different ways.

One child found some grass with dew on it. She put it up to her face to feel the wetness. She suggested other children feel it.

I will just tell you a few things the children said:

> *Michele:* Look, this is a precious thing. (It was a leaf with dew on it. It's enough to have a little sunlight and it seems like a treasure.)
> *Maria:* I found a powerful yellow!

The children discover that there are many different tonalities of color. In this case, it is the color yellow to which they assign different names. This is important to record and bring inside because giving different names to different tonalities of color means that the children understand their different identities. It is not just yellow anymore. It is a "powerful yellow" according to this child. Other children discover other yellows—light-yellow, yellow-yellow, yellow-green. . . .

The bark of the trees is always enchanting to children. Maybe because it is their height. Bark is filled with beautiful, fascinating colors. When I go out with a group of children, some are interested right away, others go to other places or run around. I think we need to give them time. There are children who come back after a little while, others who don't seem interested. Maybe they need another time.

Sometimes, we go out to notice how the color of a field changes when it is exposed to light or to shade. We might ask the children, "Are the colors the same in the light and in the shade?" Once a child took a leaf and moving back and forth from the light to the shade, almost speaking to herself she said, "Here, it lights up, here it turns off, here it lights up, here it turns off." This is a beautiful discovery.

I have noticed that 3-year-olds speak and seem very able to enjoy and understand many things outside. They say beautiful things. However, once we are inside, they don't always seem to maintain these links. Any strategies that help to maintain a strong "umbilical cord" between the experiences outside and inside are important.

Outside, they crunch through the autumn leaves. They crumple them in their hands. They make all kinds of sounds. So I bring a tape recorder so that these sounds can become a "soundtrack" that I can use while I am projecting slides or while the children work with the leaves. They can hear again and relive the experience through sound. These are ways to keep the experience they had present and alive.

The Jar Full of Earth and Sky

This is an example of a wonderful experience with 3-year-olds. Usually we collect things from outside in baskets or little sacks. This time, we asked the children to put the things they wanted to collect in a transparent jar. Laura, the teacher, told them they could collect everything they wanted, including all the colors they could see, to take back to their classmates.

The first thing that Tommy said was, "Let's put in our yells!" because they were excited and yelling. It was a lovely idea, so they yelled inside the jar closing it right away with its cover. Then, every once in a while they raised the cover ever so slightly, putting their ear to the opening to see if they could hear the yells that they had put inside. They also opened the lid to carefully add some earth. They said they wanted to put in some air and a little piece of sky. They were running everywhere. They climbed up a structure and mimed taking a piece of the sky. They smelled the odors and then breathed them into the glass. All the while, I was following this event as the photographer.

I think we need to follow the children in this exploration. It is like a great game of ping pong that we have to know how to play with them. They know how to play with us. They are clever, able, and intelligent. We have to be the same and learn how to be open in their games.

So, the jar was all closed, full of sand, earth, their calls, the sky, and the air. They came back into the class. Two days later, these children and the teachers used a few slides that I had taken to explain to the others what happened. I think this sharing with others is really an important training. They invented a way to mime to explain to the other children what they had done. Then, another day, there was a chance for a different group to make another jar of this kind. All the transparent jars remained well in view on a shelf until they deteriorated. And every now and then, the children went to stand near them remembering and noticing how the elements of the courtyard had been combined with the advancing autumn.

Using Natural Materials

A gathered leaf can serve as a piece of paper on which the children can play color games with other leaves, seeds, and flowers. We have to learn to listen to the different identities of children and address each one in a different way. My colleague, Laura, understands that each child has a different approach to doing these kind of things. She distances herself and then comes back to discuss their ideas with them. This is not a game of making colors with markers. The game is perception. Maybe this kind of a game will make them more responsive to the natural colors outside.

In this case, the children do not use glue because for some children, it can become more important than the leaves. Then, it is also important for them to try, to move, and to change the positions and compositions of the leaves. They can play for a long time making things without glue.

We realized that children also could play with different colors of earth to make other fascinating nonfigurative compositions. Different sands and soils, attractively arranged on a table, invite children to play with different kinds and colors of earth. The children make beautiful designs with the earth, which remind me of the work of African women around their houses. It is not by accident that many contemporary artists also use these natural materials. There is always a strong link between children and the time they live in history. It is a positive thing if the school can enable children to make connections with the culture of their time.

Children also can use crushed autumn leaves to play other games with color. They can try to reproduce these colors with paint. There are children who seem to forget the colors and the connections. But at a certain point, a child took a leaf and put it next to the color he was painting. Soon another child did. One child took his whole painting and put it next to the natural objects.

This is not a relationship of little importance. When a child of 3 years old realizes that the colors outside are related to paint colors, it is a big discovery and it needs to be sustained.

Teachers who are able to work this way are those teachers who are attentive. They have learned to listen to children. I think what distinguishes us in Reggio Emilia is that we have always forced ourselves to listen. I have always had the impression that I receive more from children than I give to them. We exchange enthusiasm and amazement, marvels and pleasures. That which I try to communicate always is friendship, esteem, and solidarity.

Through these images of Vea's, we are able to see how important it is to the teachers in Reggio Emilia that children notice the beauty, diversity, and detail of the natural world around them. Furthermore, teachers feel not only is it important that they notice these things, but also that it is crucial that the children find ways to remember and continue to marvel at what they discover, through expressing their ideas in many ways such as in language, in mime, in paint, in clay, and through playing with leaves and sands and soils to make small worlds and pleasing compositions.

This is not accomplished through "teaching" children to notice and to paint, but through entering into games together and sharing wonder and enthusiasm in true reciprocal relationships. The teachers listen intently to the way children perceive and understand the world and respond with both appreciation and the expertise to help them build on and expand what they understand.

CHAPTER 3

The Children and the Trees

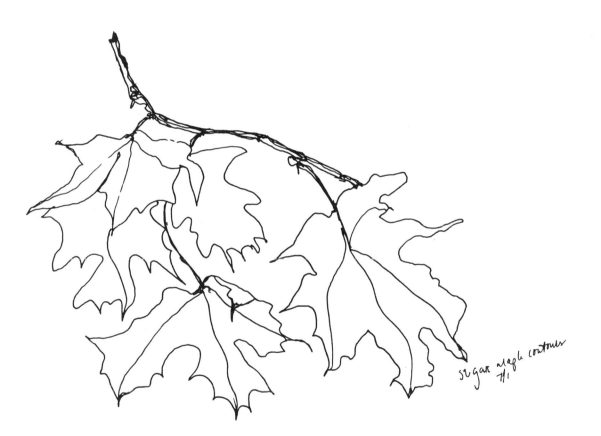

sugar maple contours
71

Yesterday, I stood under the tree where I was married 19 years ago. The majestic white pine stands firm at the top of a meadow that slopes down to an ocean inlet in Wiscasset, Maine. Its needles still whisper in the wind and glisten in the sunlight, and the scent of salt air mingles with the fragrance of pine and of ragosa rose. As I stood under its wide branches, I remembered my wedding day, walking on my father's arm, from the house toward the tree, both of us with the taste of tears in our mouths.

My father is not so strong now. He is 88 years old. He hasn't traveled to Maine for 3 years. I miss him as I begin to write about trees and I am grateful for the clear memory of a ceremony of family and friends witnessed and presided over by this guardian pine. I feel blessed by its presence in my life. I feel fortunate that it still stands here and that we can visit it and remember from time to time.

Another favorite family tree is outside my mother's bedroom porch in St. Louis, Missouri—a sour gum that she planted 20 years ago and now stretches toward the roof. It is among the last trees to turn fiery red in the fall and the last to bud out in feathery, yellow-green, baby leaves in the spring. Surrounded by double banks of windows on three sides, this porch is my mother's "moon viewing room"—a room for watching the seasons change and the cycles of the moon and stars repeat themselves through the years. From this porch, she can live in the company of the birds, the sky, and the trees.

I have long loved trees, growing up under lofty oaks in Missouri and among the pines and spruce of the Maine woods during summers as a child. My Maine memories always circle round and round to settle quietly on times shared with my mother in the forest. We walked together on the soft, pungent needles of the deep Maine woods on treasure hunts for ferns growing out of rocks, red bunch berries, and shafts of light shining down in filtered rays through tall stands of hemlock and spruce.

I think of Joseph Bruchac, an Abenaki author and storyteller who tells about walking in the woods with an elder. All of a sudden, the elder stopped and put his finger to his lips. "Can you hear it?" he whispered. Joseph listened. "Hear what?" he answered. "Can you hear what the birch leaves are saying to you?" Joseph lamented that most of us have lost the capacity to listen to what the trees and the leaves tell us. He told us that trees had long been revered by his people and the people of many cultures as wise elders who stand quietly for our rootedness in earth and our longing for the sky and the heavens.

In his introductory essay to John Sexton's book entitled *Listen to the Trees*, Stewart Udall (1994) asks:

> Should we listen [to trees] with our eyes? Ears? Hands? Considering this puzzle, we encounter another: Once listening, what are we listening for? By raising these questions, I do not mean to play word games or engage in mysticism. I am no Druid. In my opinion the colloquy between humans and trees is perfectly straight-forward. We listen to trees by paying attention to them. By heeding their grace. And, above all, appreciating what they add to our lives. The essential conversation we have with trees is not so much a path for discussion as it is an avenue for gratitude, a channel for thanksgiving. (pp. 13–15)

Two years ago, I visited the biosphere experiment in Arizona where eight men and women lived for 2 years in an enormous greenhouse to see whether they could survive in the mini-ecosystem that had been designed to imitate Biosphere One, Earth. I had a chance to talk with Linda Leigh, a botanist who had helped to design the biosphere and now lived in it. We talked with each other using telephones as we greeted each other through a thick glass window. In spite of the barrier, we were animated and excited to meet one another. Intrigued by what she had committed herself to, I asked what had impressed her most about living in the biosphere.

The first thing she said was, "I have no doubt where my life is coming from. I know where the oxygen I breath is made. I am intimately connected to the trees here, and they to me. I can feel the exchange between us."

When I arrived in Reggio Emilia in the fall of 1991, the 5-year-olds and their teachers at the Diana School were immersed in a study of trees and plants in a way that I had never witnessed before. What the children were learning had a great deal to do with both paying attention to trees and appreciating them as well as understanding their intimate connection and relationship to themselves.

Their appreciation, understanding, and strong relationship with trees was developing through their own personal experience with their own plants and their own "adopted" trees. It was also developing through talking together, wondering together, and putting their ideas together about the workings of trees and plants. The big questions that grew out of their discussions with the teachers were, What do plants and trees need to live? How do they relate to other elements and other living beings? Do they communicate? How can we communicate with them? What purpose do they serve? How do they move through the seasons? How do they "work"? As they considered these big questions, they explored many possible answers, which they drew, sculpted, wrote, spoke, and painted together.

In this chapter, I will begin by describing the way the educators in Reggio Emilia define and develop "projects." I will then tell the story of the tree project as I experienced it. The children's dialogues and work with materials become more complex as they explore both the beauty and the "workings" of trees over time. This work prepares them for their role as parents of two trees from their school yard, which they "adopt" during the latter half of the project. The course of choosing their trees, deciding how to care for them, observing their changes through the seasons, and finally celebrating one tree in grand style, is both the richest part and the culmination of their year-long study.

I often heard Loris Malaguzzi refer to projects in the Reggio Emilia preschools as "long stories"—stories that begin with a subject that is already familiar to the children in some way, but that also hold the potential for something new and exciting to happen. He said the subject needs to be a "warm" one, one that will engage the children over time. He also recommended that a project have some kind of a final objective or "destination," as he often called it. In an interview with Lella Gandini, Malaguzzi (1992) said:

> There are a few essential elements of a good project. The first is to find an initial motivation which warms up the children. There is always a sort of prologue which begins with sharing information about the theme within the group and extracting ideas from the thoughts the children have and bring to the group. Then we help the children expand their intentions and at the same time, we expand ours. . . . The ball is passed along many times. At times the children

throw it and at times we do. . . . The adults should set up situations in advance that facilitate the work of the children. The adults have to revisit what has happened, to listen a great deal and to know how to enter and how much. They have to know how to keep the children's motivation high. (pp. 2–3)

I felt particularly fortunate to join the teachers Marina Mori and Paola Strozzi and the class of the oldest children in their long investigation and growing appreciation of the trees in their lives.

HISTORY OF THE TREE PROJECT

Where did the Tree Project begin? Where did the story start? Vea Vecchi, the *atelierista* at the Diana School, explained the origin of the project to a visiting delegation from the United States in this way:

This school is in the middle of the public gardens. The gardens are encircled by trees. Every day, here in the courtyard, here in gardens, children are in the midst of the trees. In their daily life, they have continual relationships with these trees.

Before we began, the first thing we asked ourselves was: "Do the children see the trees? What kind of relationship do the children have with them? Are the trees an important presence for the children?"

Trees have been spoken about a lot lately as an important presence, but we actually do not know them very well and we are more or less inattentive to them. At the ecological, philosophical, and cultural level we use many terms but in reality these philosophies are "without blood." At a cultural, political, and economic level, we are not making significant changes in our attitude or in the way we live. The Italian ecological culture is probably less advanced than others.

Our goals and desires with this project were that the children would begin to encounter the trees with attention, with affection, and with an attitude of nurturing. At the same time, we wanted to avoid a romantic, pastoral kind of approach. We didn't want to preach about ecological issues and we wanted to avoid an excessively scientific approach.

When I came into the classroom that fall, I walked into the middle of the ongoing Tree Project. There was not a predictable sequence to follow. There was no unit plan, no weekly detailed lesson plan. The project was planned and built with the teachers and children together. I became like a detective as I began to piece together how the Tree Project started, what had happened, what was happening, and where it was going.

The project began the spring before I arrived in Reggio Emilia when these children were 4- and 5-year-olds. I knew, visitors knew, parents knew, and the children remembered what had happened the previous spring because of the panels displayed on two full walls of the 5-year-old children's classroom. When I joined the group, I could catch up on what had happened by reading the words and seeing the photographs of the children and the children's drawings and paintings, which were displayed.

The children's and teachers' experiences were not organized and presented on these panels in a linear sequence of events. Rather, the most significant events and most important discoveries that the children had made were organized and presented as such. These discoveries were made through actual encounters with the trees, through their discussions, or through their experiences with the materials that they used to represent their ideas. The first panel began with Vea's introduction.

> Representation is never a reproduction of reality, but a co-production between the author and the reality represented. This co-production is made possible through the experience, imagination, graphic training, memories, and sensations of the artist or author.
>
> The tree becomes "visible" only through a rich contextual network. This network includes the child who perceives the tree, which presents itself to the child. This tree is never static, but always changing.
>
> We have introduced the tree to the child and the child to the tree in a way in which the child is able to see the tree as a vital entity with its own narrative. While the child sees and touches the tree, draws the buds, the leaves, the bark, the fallen trunk, the roots, the branches, he or she gradually sees, touches, and draws parts of a living organism, the parts of which are all related, important, and known as friends. The relationship between the child and tree becomes a real-life relationship.

Vea's introduction summarizes the arguments of Lowenfeld (1964) and Burton (1991) that we do not paint or draw objects in the world but rather paint and draw our relationship with them. Because the way in which the children meet the trees and begin to discover them is exceedingly rich, the "relationships" that they are then able to draw and paint are equivalently rich.

From reading the panels and viewing the photographs and the children's work, I was able to trace how the Tree Project began and developed: A group of boys and girls went out in the spring to explore a sycamore tree in front of the school. They explored the feel of the bark, the animal skin patterns of the bark, the emerging buds, the smells of the tree, and the shadow cast by the tree.

The children and teachers followed the initial exploration with a discussion on the parts of the tree the children had discovered. One panel included transcriptions of the children's language (comments, ideas, hypotheses) divided into the categories of the buds and the bark of the tree. It included close-up drawings and photographs of clay representations of the buds.

Another panel displayed a montage of children's life-sized, detailed pen drawings of leaves in many shades of greens. Yet another panel included tempera paintings of bark. The drawings and clay representations of buds, the leaf drawings, and the bark paintings all began with children's close observations of these parts of the tree.

With the encouragement of their teachers, children often work "from life" in the schools here. In this way, they develop their ability to notice and to enter into relationships with another being or object. At the same time, they grow in their capacity to invent ways to express varieties and subtleties of line, texture, shape, form, and color with many different materials.

The kind of documentation developed here often emphasizes the process—the words, the actions, the spoken thoughts of a child or of a small group, while working with the materials—in order to reveal the child's point of view, the path a child or a group has taken to arrive at a solution, and the child's way of thinking, sensing, feeling, and working. For example, another panel described the children's discovery of several ways to make a tree trunk of clay stand upright.

Children's drawings, which illustrated their ideas about the tree and how it might feel and look in various situations, were displayed on another panel. One drawing showed a tree "in anger when the wind comes because it has to hold on tight and the wind blows too hard." Vea told me that, as teachers, they have noticed that the children's schema of the tree, or their way of drawing a tree (or another subject), often changes considerably when the ideas of movement or relationship come up, for example, the tree in relationship with the wind or the rain or the sun.

This idea of relationship is a basic tenet of the Reggio Approach. Trees are not static. They are in constant movement, change, and relationship with other elements. The educators in Reggio Emilia believe that young children flourish when they are challenged and supported in discovering this complex net of relationships. The educators here continually ask children to notice, think about, create, and express their unique perspective on relationships of all kinds through many languages.

The last panel in the documentation of the Tree Project included small photographs of the children's trip to a greenhouse in June. They went to see how plants get their start and how a greenhouse works. While they were there, they each chose a plant to take home for the summer to care for as their own. The photographs communicate all this as well as the delight of the children together in the midst of the rich soil and the new, young plants.

A booklet entitled "Plants Are Planted with Their Feet Under the Ground" was put together for the children to take home with their plants for the summer. It contained the children's ideas and drawings arranged into chapters: the leaves, the roots (the little legs of life), the rights of plants, the illnesses and dangers to plants, the friends of the plants, plants and the rain, plants and the wind, the birds, the feelings of the plants.

The first page includes a list of all the authors of the text and the graphics, the children of the Diana School, section B. The booklet begins with a letter "to the families" from the teachers Vea, Marina, and Magda.

> If we grew up primarily in the city, we probably remember experiences like watching a bean sprout in wet cotton or watering geraniums on the balcony. For many of us, the relationship we have with the natural world has not developed much beyond these first encounters. This profound lack of knowledge cannot help but impoverish us.
>
> On the other hand, it seems easier for us to feel close to a domestic animal like a dog or cat who shares some fundamental social relationships we do (for example, sexual and familial). We tend to feel we are more distant from the plant world.
>
> The proposal to the children to take care of a plant during the period of the vacation will allow them to become close to a form of life

very different from ours, but with which we think it is possible to establish relationships. The early development of a real, and not rhetorical, environmental consciousness can take its start in this way: simply by taking care of a plant.

      To the parents: A warning—the sense of great responsibility that the child can derive from being the custodian of a living thing requires the closeness of an attentive and sensitive adult who believes this is an important activity.

      At the end of the summer vacation the plant will return to school with the child and the presence of "green" in the classroom will surely be less anonymous.

In this way, the teachers work with the parents on continuing summer experiences that relate to what has been going on at school. The teachers felt the children could expand their understanding about the trees and the plant world by taking care of a small part of that world. It was a way to link the plant project with summertime activities and with parents.

      I came into the 5- and 6-year-old room at the end of September 1992, when most of the plants had come back to school, some very healthy and some not so healthy. The plants were placed around the room in various windows.

PLANTS IN RELATIONSHIPS

The first part of the project that I actually witnessed was a series of discussions with groups of four children and Marina Mori. These discussions were in preparation for pairs of children to draw their plants in relationship with each other. The idea that plants communicate among themselves and with others had emerged during a previous discussion among the children.

      Marina asked questions as starting points for another discussion about the plants in relationship to other elements—for example, people, other plants, noise, light, insects. Vea explained to me that for discussions such as this one, the teachers often prepare a series of questions to use if the opportunity arises. They do not intend to use all the questions, but rather to be prepared with a variety of possibilities, which, in turn, have been prompted by the children's previous ideas. However, they are ready to take other directions if the children take the discussion elsewhere. Here are some of the questions Marina and Vea prepared:

- Some of you have said that plants do not like to be by themselves and that they prefer company. What do you think of this?
- Do they prefer silence or noise?
- Do you think they like being around a lot of children?
- Of what use are the roots to the plants?
- What do you think plants eat?
- Do you think they prefer light or dark? Why?
- Are there other beings that go near plants? Do they bother the plants?
- Do the plants have friends or enemies? Who are they?
- Do plants show emotions? Which ones?

- Do plants communicate? With whom? In what way?
- Who decides which type, size, and color the plant will be?

These open-ended questions are typical of the kinds of questions asked by the teachers in the Reggio Emilia preschools. They are not asked to elicit right answers, but rather to stimulate children to think, imagine, remember, make comparisons, and formulate new ideas. They are asked in the spirit of exploration. They are asked by a teacher who wants to go on a journey with the children and their ideas. I later learned that most often these questions grow out of previous experiences and discussions between teachers and children and that a number of teachers usually work together to decide on the best questions for a particular discussion and the best way to ask them.

Conversations with Children About Their Plants

The following is an excerpt from the conversation between Marina and a small group: Ale, Marco, Maria Guilia, and Francesca, ages 5 to 5.5 (see Figure 3.1).

Marina: When you returned to school after the summer, where did you put your plant?
Ale: Near Cecilia's.
Marina: Ale, do you think your plant is happy near Cecilia's plant?

FIGURE 3.1. A Small Group Conversation About Plants

Ale: They are all plants. They are all the same. They like each other's company.

Marina: Do you think these plants are happier here at school or at your houses?

Ale: Mine is happier at home because I give it food. But it is also happy here.

Marina: Why is that?

Ale: Because it's happy when you come near because it thinks you are going to give it water. If you don't come near, it will think that you aren't a friend anymore.

Maria Guilia: I think the plants are happy here because now we're here.

Marina: So, when we all go home, how do you think the plants feel?

Ale: They are better off when we're here, because we're their owners and we give them water and food.

Marina: Ale, you always have beautiful things to say, but you need to let the others talk, too. Do you think the plants like the dark or light better?

Maria Guilia: They like light because if they stayed in the dark, they'd die.

Ale: They like sun because they don't want to be alone in the dark.

Marina: Is there another reason they like the light, other than not wanting to be alone?

Maria Guilia: They suffer in the dark. They can't see. They would die. They need a little light.

Marina: What does the light do? If we took a plant and put it in a room without light ever in the day . . .

Ale: It would die. It would get tired without eating, without anything, because the light feeds it.

Maria Guilia: It would get dry.

Marco: The leaves would fall.

Francesca: It would get black.

Marina: Let's go near the plants. Are there other creatures that go near plants?

Marco: Insects, like bees, flies, and mosquitoes, which tickle them.

Marina: Would you like to try to draw your plant in relationship with something else: another plant, the plant of your friend, an insect, someone who is watering the plant . . . you decide.

Marco: Let's make plants who love each other.

Ale: No, they are getting married.

Marina: You need to decide together what your two plants are doing . . . agree among yourselves. Remember the roots. Remember that last year you called them "the little legs of life."

Here is another excerpt from a later conversation between Marina and another group on the same subject, plants in relationship. Omar, Agnese, and Elisa are also ages 5 to 5.5.

Marina: Agnese, what happened to your plant?

Agnese: I put it near the heater at home, and that was it, all the leaves fell off. It was too hot.

Marina: In your opinion, are our plants inside our class happy here? Do they like children?

Agnese: If we give them water and food, yes.

Omar: They'll die without water, also if we don't give them fertilizer.

Marina: What is fertilizer?

Agnese: It's pasta for them, not for us. Little black pellets, it makes them do
        well.

Marina: How do you think they eat and drink?

Agnese: Through their roots. They are like our tonsils.

Marina: What do the roots look like?

Agnese: Very thin. Also fat and even thinner. If the branches are big, the roots
        are also big. They are attached to the branches; otherwise only the roots
        would eat.

Marina: And later, what do the plants do?

Agnese: They make little leaves and new branches and stems.

Elisa: Also they get bigger and bigger.

Marina: Do you think they prefer light or dark?

Agnese: If they're always in the dark, they won't grow.

Elisa: They get a little bored in the dark. They want to get to know each other.

Marina: And how do plants get to know each other?

Omar: They need to be close. Their roots can also get to know each other.

Marina: How could you draw your plants in relationship?

Agnese: Your plant can be the plant doctor, Elisa, and tell my plant what it
        needs to do.

Although I was fascinated with the children's ideas, I began to wonder
about the questions that attributed feelings to the plants. They seemed to be
leading the children astray or away from "scientifically correct" thinking. Were
the teachers helping the children learn about plants or were they encouraging
fantasy? When I asked Marina about this, she reminded me that the questions
had grown out of previous discussions in which the children had repeatedly
spoken about the thoughts and feelings of the plants. Perhaps, not to attribute
feelings to the plants would be unnatural for them. She added that recent scientific studies had demonstrated that certain plants did flourish when they were
talked to gently and when soft music was played. Maybe the children's ideas
were not so far from reality. I realized that Marina's questions actually were
related to the life of the plants. Through further discussions with Vea, I learned
that to the educators in Reggio Emilia, animism is not negative, or merely a stage
of childhood thought, but rather an approach to the world that offers a way to
enter into relationship with that which is considered different than we are.

As I witnessed more and more conversations, I began to understand the
many ways in which children think and go about expressing their ideas in response to open-ended questions about things and phenomena that catch their
interest and imagination. I also began to appreciate what we, as adults, can learn
about children and from children if we ask the right questions, which are in tune
with their ideas, and are able to listen to their responses with our complete
attention.

In an introductory pamphlet given to all visitors as an introduction to the
schools, the educators in Reggio Emilia affirm that

> Children are . . . detectives, gifted with the capacity to utilize clues, to hypothe-
> size "missing" explanations and to reconstruct facts. From the very beginning,
> their curiosity in learning refuses simple and isolated things. Instead, children

love to find the dimensions and relations of complex situations, . . . create analogies, metaphors, anthropomorphic meanings, and logical meanings.

This conversation about plants reveals this kind of curiosity and thinking
at work. Because teachers and children regularly engage in this kind of dialogue
together, they become accustomed to the exchange of ideas between children
and between children and teachers. They both find great pleasure in this practice. The recorded conversations become the core of their ongoing explorations
and project work together.

The Plant Drawings

In this case, the conversation was a strong motivation and preparation for the
children to further their thinking about plants in relationships through drawing.
The teachers and children agreed that the drawings could be done in collaboration with a friend if the children wished. The proposal to the children was not
simply to describe their plant or to draw their plant, but rather to think of their
plant in a net of relationships with the other plants and other elements, to
discuss these ideas with other children, to choose an idea to represent, and then
to draw it alongside another child. The plan of the teacher was not to "teach"
concepts of ecology or biology or to give an art lesson, but rather to provide a
challenging, supportive context in which the children's own ideas could grow
(see Figure 3.2).

The following two examples represent the kinds of drawings that children did after participating in the plant conversations. Cecilia and Luca decide
to draw their two plants as plants who love each other and are reaching out to
one another in an embrace (see Figure 3.3). They each drew curving lines with
circles and zig-zag lines to represent their plants' stems and leaves. They have
connected the stem lines so that the two plants become one in the center. This
is similar to the way in which children sometimes draw themselves holding a
friend's hand. They actually share a hand.

Elisa decided to work alone because she wanted to draw her plant in
relationship to the sun and the rain (see Figure 3.4). Elisa uses the same lines,
circles, and zig-zags, yet she is able to use them in a more sophisticated way than
Cecilia or Luca. She observes and draws the way the stems on her plant bend
and the way the leaves are formed. She carefully adds the veins in each leaf and
the roots inside the pot. She uses short lines to represent rain falling on the plant.
She uses the technique that cartoonists use to indicate dreaming by making a
wiggley connecting line from the leaves to the sun in the left-hand corner. In
fact, her plant is "in the rain dreaming of the sun."

Painting Leaves

As the rotating groups of children were drawing their plants in relationships,
each child had a chance (over a period of about a month) to work at the easel in
tempera to paint leaves or other parts of their plants. Children chose between
rectangular neutral or colored tissue paper and selected their own paint colors
from a cart of prepared colors—five or six gradations each of yellows, blues,
violets, greens, and earth tones.

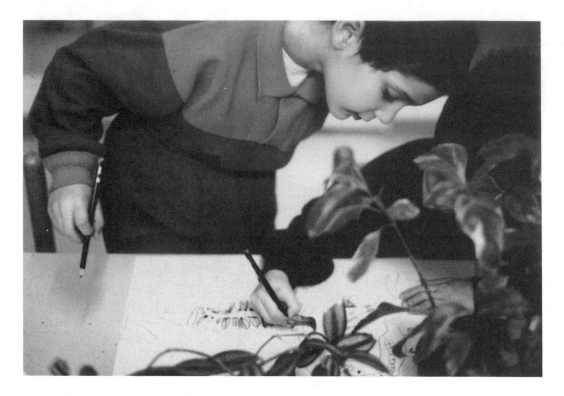

FIGURE 3.2.   Drawing Plants in Pairs

Agnese was the first to begin. Marina asked her to choose her paper. Agnese said, "I'd like yellow. Then it will be like the sun, don't you think?"

Later, I watched Maria Giulia paint. Earlier, when she was with the small group in the mini-*atelier*, I had watched her tenderly caress the leaves of her plant before she drew it. She seemed to paint with the same tenderness and attentive care (see Figure 3.5).

I watched several other children work quite independently on their paintings, with suggestions every once in a while from Marina. For example, "Have you noticed all the greens in the leaf you are painting? You can take the colors you want and change colors when you need to."

These children have used tempera paint independently for 3 years at the Diana School. Last year, some children made enlarged paintings of bark and cross-sections of a tree trunk. Now, they use the paint and brushes with ease, familiarity, and great pleasure.

Clay, Branches, Bark

I spent several days in the mini-*atelier* with groups of four to six children following the same theme of plants and trees in relationship to other things, only this time the children used clay and wood as the medium.

I asked Vea where the idea of the clay and wood came from. She said, "In a sense, ideas come from everywhere—from contemporary art, from films, from looking around you, from reading, . . . and, of course, from what the children say and do. Clay and wood are both natural materials. It comes very naturally to children to combine these and other materials.''

Marina began by putting pieces of bark and small fallen branches, which had been collected on outings with children, on the mini-*atelier* table and conversing with the children about possibilities for the day. She reminded them of conversations they had about insects and little animals living on and in the trees. She asked, ''Would you like to make branches and leaves in clay near these wooden branches, or insects that could be walking on the bark?''

Matteo chose to make ants. Marina found him some photographs of ants to refer to if he wanted to. He made a family of them. They were not detailed ant bodies, but small pinched pieces of red clay with smaller pieces attached for legs and tiny indented eyes made with a small pointed tool. He asked Marina to identify the ants on a written label, ''The first one is doing somersaults, the second one is jumping, the third one is standing on his hind legs, and the last one is taking a bath.''

Luca and Lorenzo chose to work together to make vines and leaves of clay around a branch. A few days later, I watched Elisa carefully trace the outlines of a large sycamore leaf she had brought in from the gardens onto a slab

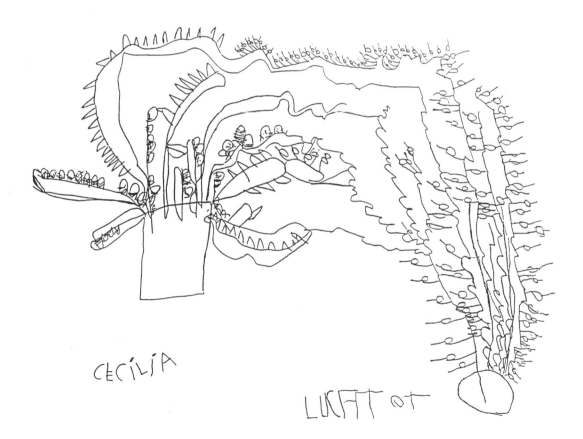

FIGURE 3.3. Luca and Cecilia's Drawing

FIGURE 3.4.   Elisa's Drawing

of clay. After cutting it out of the slab, she drew the veins of the leaf into the clay with great attention (see Figure 3.6). She had the leaf beside her as well as an enlarged photocopy of a magnified leaf that showed the cells and veins, which Marina had given her from a file of resources. The clay leaf later joined another leaf and several insects inside a large coil pot that she and her friend Agnese made over several days in the mini-*atelier*.

As the children worked, Marina observed and took notes, writing down what the children said. From time to time, she suggested that they look more closely to further define a part or relationship between parts. Many of her suggestions to look closely were based on the structure and function of the plant or insect. For example, "If the veins of the leaf are all mixed up like that, how will the water get to all the parts?" or "If the legs of the ant are so heavy, how will he walk?"

I was struck by the ability of these 5-year-old children to make insects and leaves from clay. They often used photographs or photocopies of scientific drawings of leaves, insects, snails, or small animals from the file to work from.

FIGURE 3.5. Painting Plants

FIGURE 3.6. Making Leaf Portraits Out of Clay

These photographs offered another perspective on the real leaves they also used as models. They used pointed tools to make the veins and to define parts of the insects. They knew how to use slip (a mixture of clay and water) to attach pieces of clay together. They were familiar with ways to form and to work with both slabs and coils.

As with drawing materials and with paint, the children here have had many opportunities to play and to work with clay in many different contexts. Now, they know many of the possibilities as well as the limitations of clay as a medium. They can use it with skill to express their growing knowledge, their fanciful ideas, and their developing relationship with the trees and plants around them. Some children were more able than others, but all seemed to derive satisfaction and pleasure from working from life to make something so alive in clay.

WHY DO YOU THINK THE TREES ARE IMPORTANT TO US?

All of the experiences described so far happened in the autumn before the winter holiday. A book entitled ''The Roots Hold the Tree Tight to Life,'' including many of the children's ideas and theories about plants and trees in words and drawings, was given to the parents by the children at the annual Christmas holiday party. These ideas came from a series of discussions teachers and children had before Christmas.

After their return in January, Vea, Marina, and Paola reviewed this book to look for children's ideas that were particularly rich—ideas that would be valuable to revisit with the children so that they might extend them, enrich them, or connect them to other ideas through some of the other "hundred languages." Among others, they selected the following children's ideas in response to the question: Why do you think the trees and plants are important to us?

- Certain trees are interesting because they are beautiful and of all colors and because of this we like them a lot.
- Without trees the birds couldn't build their nests, and they would be all eaten up by the cats.
- Leaves, roots, branches, and plants are very important to man because they are very beautiful and they also take the bad smoke in and spit out good air.
- Without plants, we wouldn't have fruit or vegetables or vitamins, which help us grow and are good for us . . . and mothers, what would they do to make babies?
- The trees are important because they take away the smoke of the cars. They move their leaves, and they take away the smoke.
- We couldn't live without them, because they give us oxygen. It's oxygen that commands the brain. The trees take in air and then they give us oxygen.

The opportunity to make an idea come alive visually is exciting and challenging to the children. It helps the children better understand their own ideas and other children's ideas because they can see them, feel them, hold them, sometimes walk around them (sculpture), or even hear them (moving or sound sculpture). In response to a question about the relationship between words and visual symbols for children, Malaguzzi (1992) said:

> [To make a visual symbol, children] need to reflect on the meaning of words in order to give them a more concrete form. They must be selective . . . and then transfer dominant concepts to graphic means. To make a statement (graphically) is to make concretely visible what so far has been part of the flood of spoken language . . . [and it] also means the children understand that their [drawings] must be tools of communication. (pp. 6–7)

The teachers discuss with the children what might be the best material or combination of materials to communicate a particular idea. The following examples show how two of the collective ideas were "recycled" in very different ways as well as used to provoke further thinking and new ideas.

"The Trees Are Important Because They Are Beautiful."

One morning, while Marina was working with a small group of four in the mini-*atelier*, Paola proposed to the rest of the children (approximately 18) that they each draw a tree with whatever colored pens they might want, to represent the idea that the trees are beautiful, different, and of many colors. They took a moment to look outside at all the varieties of trees in the public gardens they could see from the classroom windows.

Then, for approximately 45 minutes, very independently, each child invented an extraordinary, fanciful, unusual tree. Paola told me that her only input was to continue to comment on how beautiful and unique the drawings were as they began to emerge. Again, I was impressed by the children's ability, by the beauty and originality of each drawing, and by the apparent ease and pleasure with which each child drew his or her tree (see Plate 2).

When I shared this observation with Vea, Marina, and Paola, they all thought it was not so unusual. They said, "We provided pens of all kinds of colors . . . we asked them to look at and think about trees being different." Marina did tell me that she thought the children's close involvement with the real trees allowed them to be more fantastic in their creations of the "beautiful trees." She also said she did not feel the children separated the imaginary trees much from the trees they drew or painted or sculpted *dal vero* (from life).

In this particular case, the graphic material was a wide range of very good-quality magic marker pens, thin and fat, with many choices of colors, on white paper. These children have had many opportunities to use these kinds of pens in many different situations during their 3 years at the Diana School.

For example, while I was at both the Diana and La Villetta Schools, I saw marker pens used most often by the children to make a "game of colors," which is just that: colors used to make free-form, playful designs. Vea and Marina tell me they notice that particularly at age 4, children begin to enjoy this kind of playing with colors side by side, watching their designs take form and change. They say it is important to continue to value this kind of playing with colors alongside the children's growing ability and interest in drawing figuratively.

During my career as a teacher, I have seen children invent "color games" many times; however, I have never seen the idea so supported and encouraged on a daily basis. I have never given this form of drawing a name or suggested these designs as additions to children's messages or letters. Because the color games are a part of their daily life, valued and encouraged, these children continue to develop a strong sense of color and design and to derive a great deal of pleasure in their creations.

It seems to me that the daily familiarity with the possibilities of the material (good-quality markers), the association with color play (manifest in the strength of design and pattern in each tree drawing), the excitement of using the rich colors to draw beautiful trees, as well as their close and ever-growing relationship with the trees around them, made it possible for each child to create what would become one of a forest of beautiful trees. The trees, in fact, were all mounted on cardboard and cut out to stand up, so together they would become a forest of beautiful, different, fantastic trees of all colors, representing the children who created them.

"The Trees Suck in the Bad Air and Spit Out the Good Air."

This was the second recycled idea or theory that was "tossed back" to the children. Because she knew they were particularly interested in the idea and in clay as a medium, Marina asked Bobo and Marco if they would like to use clay to represent their ideas about the trees spitting out the good air.

Marina, Bobo, and Marco discussed together various ways of using the clay and decided on a low relief. Using the clay in a flat format would provide them with a background on which to represent the air. The three of them considered this. They agreed that it might be more difficult to represent the good air with a three-dimensional standing clay sculpture. So, they chose the low relief this time and for this case.

The boys began to build up their trunk, branches, and leaves with small bits of clay on a clay plaque that they prepared. When they got to the air, Marina asked them, "What is clean air like?" They said, "Blue." They asked if they could use blue glaze in two gradations—a light blue and a darker blue. I watched them take turns using a small brush to apply the glaze, coaching each other as to what kind of brush strokes to use and where they should go. The blues wafted out of the leaves and filled the rounded square of the plaque.

Two other children, Lorenzo and Chiara, made the plaque to represent the tree taking in the bad air. This time, instead of a color, they used wire mesh and other clay tools to scratch into the clay to create agitated, slashing marks to represent "bad air." They also etched into the clay a small car emitting fumes.

This is an example of another one of the myriad ways to recycle the ideas children have expressed, or, as the Italian educators say, "toss back the ideas" to the children. This idea of the trees taking in bad air and spitting out good air was expressed by several children. It became a collective idea. Bobo and Marco were two boys particularly interested in the idea and in continuing to work in clay. Their teacher suggested they work together. She also wanted other children to be involved, and to involve one of the girls, as she had expressed this idea too.

Bobo and Marco made unusually informed choices together as to what materials and tools to use and how to use them to represent and express their ideas. Again, it seems they have developed this level of skill and facility during the 3 years at the Diana School. They have been asked what they think. They have had their ideas "tossed back" at them many times. They have learned "the alphabet and the language" of clay through many encounters of many different kinds. They have worked in pairs, worked in groups, solved their own problems, while they have followed the course of many projects. They are fulfilled by both the process they follow and the results they achieve.

"Maybe the Power Is in the Seed?!"

In reviewing what had been done with Marina several days after the plaques were completed, Vea suggested that perhaps the children could go deeper still with their ideas. She suggested to Marina that they ask the children how in the world they thought the trees could perform this "air exchange."

So Marina threw back the idea to Bobo, Marco, and now Ale, who had joined them. She asked the boys, "How do you think the trees take in the bad air and spit out the good air?"

Vea explained to me later that the boys thought for a long time without saying anything. Marco finally suggested that maybe it was the roots that exchanged the air. And then Ale said that, in his opinion, the power to exchange the air was in the seed.

The other boys liked that idea. They added, with excitement, "It starts out little, and then the power grows as the tree grows. . . . The power is passed from the seed to the trunk to the branches, to the leaves!"

Vea asked them if they would like to make the seed in clay. "That will just be a ball of clay," Bobo replied. "You can open the seed, though, and imagine what is inside," Vea suggested. "I saw a tiny, tiny leaf inside a seed once," Marco offered.

So the boys were left to make their seeds on their own. After a little while they came to Vea with several seeds of clay (a little smaller than golf balls) and said, "Open them—Vea, open the seeds." Marco and Bobo had emptied the inside of the little balls of clay to make room for tiny clay trees complete with leaves and roots. "We put the little tree in a cradle. It is this little tree that gives power to the big tree . . . and in this seed (pointing to another clay ball), we have put two little trees so as to give the tree a super power" (see Figure 3.7). As Vea commented later, these children have come upon the idea of DNA.

These are seeds of ideas, complex and complicated ideas that these boys have the opportunity to search for, intuit, and give form to. As Vea pointed out, the idea that the seed has the power, structure, and "information" inside it to grow into an adult tree is close to the biological explanation that DNA is part of the seed and holds the possibility and potentiality for the seed's growth.

In this part of the Tree Project, one can trace the children's initial ideas in first conversations into a second conversation about materials, into clay, back into thinking and hypothesizing in words, and then back into clay. The first process causes the next, and then the next, like ever-widening concentric circles caused by a pebble dropped in a pond. In this case the initial pebble dropped was the question, "Why do you think the trees are important to us?"

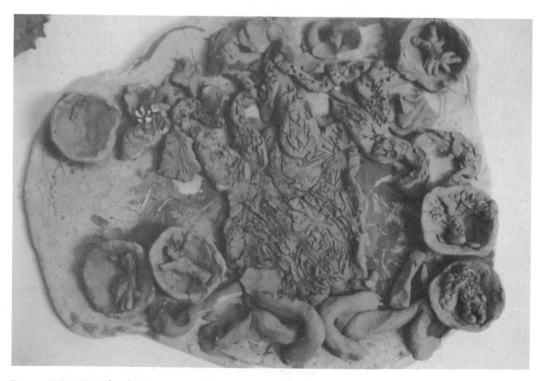

FIGURE 3.7.   "Maybe the Power is in the Seed": A Theory in Clay

TAKING STOCK OF THE WORK SO FAR

Although he was officially retired, Loris Malaguzzi was a frequent presence at the Diana School and was involved there as a master *pedagogista*. I feel extraordinarily fortunate to have known Malaguzzi personally and to have lived alongside him on a daily basis (or, as Malaguzzi might say, "in our everyday clothes instead of our Sunday clothes") as he worked with teachers, and *pedagogisti*, and hosted visitors from many countries. One of my strongest memories is of Malaguzzi working with teachers at the Diana and La Villetta Schools: shirt sleeves rolled up, brow furrowed, thinking, reading transcripts, looking at drawings, tirelessly reviewing ideas.

One winter Saturday morning Malaguzzi, Vea, Marina Mori, and I met in the mini-*atelier* of the 5-year-old room at the Diana School. Marina and Vea wanted his response to the work so far and his ideas about where they might go. We looked at children's richly detailed drawings of trees, examined their theories in clay, and read transcripts of conversations.

He looked at the work, followed the ideas, and then challenged them. He said that all the work was good, but that he thought that the children needed more encounters with the real trees. They all agreed. They discussed possible ways to move forward. There was heated discussion and some disagreement. They spent all morning at it. In the end, they decided they would suggest to the children that they adopt a nearby tree and perhaps plant a tree in their courtyard. Vea also had more ideas about combining clay and wood to make a final "tree monument."

Like the encounters between teachers, this meeting of *pedagogista*, teacher, and *atelierista* was meant to be challenging, honest, reflective. They know that, above all, they are all constantly striving to grow, learn, and evolve as educators. They want to ask themselves questions that can spiral in many directions, take them deeper, just as they hope to do with the questions they ask the children. They take time to take stock, look at what they have done, what the children have done, what is missing, and how they might proceed. The ideas and reflections come from working this process through together, and from challenging each other.

The level of confrontation during this process of reflection and planning is much more intense than I have experienced in the United States. I would guess that, in part, this is a cultural difference between Italians and Americans. In the case of the Reggio Emilia educators, they know they are all searching and trying to improve together. They are very frank with each other, yet they are not defensive. They are accepting of suggestions for improving. The discussion may appear heated at times, but it is always open.

THE ADOPTION OF TWO TREES

I was not present at the Diana School for several months during the time when the trees were being adopted because I had moved to La Villetta School for the second term of my internship. However, I was able to visit at least one day a week in the spring so I could catch up and continue to follow the project. The following story of the tree adoptions is taken from informal conversations with Vea and from a presentation she made on the project to a visiting delegation in the spring of 1994. These are Vea's words as I have transcribed and translated them.

At this point, we asked the children if they wanted to adopt a tree. While the idea was offered by adults to the children, what tree they wanted to adopt, how and why, what this would mean, would be up to them.

We asked them if they knew what it meant to adopt a tree. They said, "To take one like a daughter or son, to be a parent." They added that you would need to have an attitude of care and nurturing to adopt someone.

We went outside with four girls who were most interested in the idea. They looked at all the trees and picked a little one in the midst of two larger ones. They said, "This one is just right. It has birds. It can hold nests. It has buds. It has a trunk. It is not a rugged tree. It needs us. We have to protect it. What can we do to help the tree and the trees around it understand that we have adopted it?" They then decided to involve the other girls in the class.

We followed them. We followed the lead of the children even more so than we do in most projects. They asked all the other girls if they wanted to take care of this tree. Then they developed ideas about what they would like to do for the tree as they adopted it and what they could do to let others know it was under their care. "We want to make nests, so they will attract the birds. We want to make some clay birds to hang in the tree to keep the tree company. They will be like dolls for the tree. And we want to make a sign that says that this is the tree adopted by the girls of class C and that other children should be careful not to hurt it."

Several girls worked together to make the nests, researching the sorts of materials several birds actually use in nest making. They used clay for the base of the nests. Another small group worked on the clay birds, and another on what to write on the sign.

Carla, who can read and write, served as the scribe for the sign. The girls wondered if the tree was masculine or feminine, because they wanted to give it a name. Since no one seemed to know, she suggested they call in a tree "gynecologist" to help them determine the answer.

A father who was an agronomist and friend of the school agreed to come by to talk to the girls. In answer to their question, he explained that almost all trees are both masculine and feminine and need to be pollinated by other trees. The girls were amazed as he explained the pollination process.

They also wanted to know what they needed to do to take care of the tree, and how the tree would know that they loved it. In a later discussion, Agnese said that she felt sure the tree, being another living being, must be capable of understanding them in some way. She added that the birds must be able to communicate with the trees, living so close to them.

The girls were worried that all the children in the school generally were so excited when they were playing outside that they would not stop to read their sign. They realized the younger children would not be able to read it and would need to rely on teachers or older children who could read to them what the sign said. Because communication through letters and messages is part of their daily life at school, they thought that the children and the teachers would not ignore a hand-delivered letter. Therefore, a group of girls decided to write a letter to all the children in the school asking them to be particularly careful of their tree.

They decided in the course of writing this letter that they would name their tree Mil. They learned from the "tree gynecologist" that their tree was an apple tree. Apple in Italian is *la mela*, which is feminine. The apple tree, however, is *il melo*, which is masculine. They decided that since the tree was neither masculine nor feminine, they should drop the last letter, which indicates the gender of the word, and call their tree Mel. Then they decided to change it to Mil because they thought the name had a more pleasing ring to it. The letter read:

Dear Children of section A, B, and C,

We are the girls in section C. Do you know that we have adopted a tree in our play area outside the school? It is near the little merry-go-round. You will recognize it because there is a picture of all of the girls from our section on the tree. Children, please don't kick this tree or harm it in any way! Otherwise the tree will think that we are bad and that we are hitting it. It is a very important tree because it is an apple tree. This means it is a tree that loses its leaves, which means that now it is bare but in a very short time, in the spring, the leaves will grow again. If you are good, when it makes fruit, we will give you each a piece.

"Ciao" from the girls of section "C"

At this point, the boys decided that they wanted to adopt a tree as well. After having toured the courtyard they stopped in front of a very tall pine. They said, "This is a good one. It is the king of the trees. And, it is clever—it is never naked." Their reasons were, "It is an evergreen and it won't lose its leaves. The branches come right down to the ground and we like to play under them. We can see it from our classroom." When asked what they would like to do to indicate that it was their tree, they sang out, "Let's make a flag!"

They had a series of grand ideas. They wanted to make a pond, a bridge, traps, and signs. They divided themselves and proceeded with much excitement and grand gestures. Facing the enormity of the tasks, they accomplished only a few, but were very satisfied. They decided they must take turns guarding the tree over lunch hour.

We invited all the children to make a forest out of clay. At this point, they were happy to work together rather than separately. They enjoyed this opportunity to work together to create a woods out of clay with lots of little animals who visit, lizards, snails, birds, and families having a picnic. The trees were now entering into relationship with other living beings.

At the same time, we decided together to work with clay around a large stump of a tree found in the public garden to bring the tree back to life in a sense, with roots, branches, leaves, and little animals. Here there is the paradox of bringing the dead to life. The children thought maybe it would become alive again in a game of magic. In another sense it was like the Egyptian custom of providing all the things the dead person (in this case the tree) might need in the afterlife (nests, leaves, birds).

At last, Mil began to bloom. The children said, "Mil is the bloomingest tree in the world." In observing what happened during the process when the blossoms turned to fruit, they said, "The flowers will die and the apples will come. The apple will be the child of the flowers. The blossoms don't have a chance to see their children." Often, if the emotion becomes too strong, the children withdraw, saying, "The flower and petals are so light and fragile, their death is light. It is not heavy like our death." Malaguzzi used to say that the children perceive and express the qualities of these transformations with extremely poetic words. Even in the moments of death and transformation, they perceive the "whispers" and subtleties of phenomena.

Their understanding was growing. What is important is the two worlds in relationship to each other—the world of the trees and the world of the children, coming together until the children make all the relationships possible between themselves and the trees.

The girls decided to have a big party. They wanted to give a party for Mil and give Mil gifts. They said they wanted to give the tree gifts for both its masculine and feminine parts. For the masculine part of the tree they made insects and lizards out of clay. For the feminine part of the tree they made clay bracelets and earrings with which they adorned Mil. They wanted to give portraits of themselves and of Mil to the tree as they often do for each other on their birthdays.

Then, they began to organize the party. At first, they wanted to invite the entire city, but after discussing it, they decided to reduce the guest list. They decided, instead, to organize the party for all the children in the school. Because it rained, they had their party inside, with their best dresses and dress-ups. There were waitresses, entertainment, and singing all provided by the children of section C. They all gave messages to Mil. Two messages read, "I want to give you music that makes leaves dance in the wind," and "I want to give you the gift of rain." Their messages are full of hope and expectation to Mela, Mil, the little promise of the continuity of life [see Figure 3.8].

The adoptions of the nearby trees and all the ideas that unfolded through the work of the children and the teachers together proved to be a wonderful way to bring the children and the trees into closer relationship. As Vea stated in her introduction to the project written for the panel displays, the children now know personally the parts of the tree and its transformations through the seasons. They know Mil as a friend. This is a relationship that they will not forget.

FIGURE 3.8. The Celebration for Mil

CHAPTER 4

Returning Home to St. Louis

3/29/94
forsythia on the light table—
faculty meeting in the
preschool

It was through a remarkable turn of events that I was invited to return to my hometown of St. Louis, Missouri, to work with a group of teachers from a consortium of schools to study and attempt to adapt the principles and practices of the Reggio Approach.

In the fall of 1991, while my family and I were in Reggio Emilia, the exhibition of children's and educators' work from Reggio Emilia entitled "The Hundred Languages of Children" opened in St. Louis. As I explained in the Prologue, the exhibit and accompanying seminars created tremendous interest in the Reggio Approach. In the spring of 1992, Brenda Fyfe of Webster University led a delegation of teachers and administrators on a study tour to the Reggio Emilia preschools.

A group of five parents and teachers from the College School were among the 40 participants. They were so impressed with what they saw and with my interest in working with teachers in the United States who wished to adapt the Reggio Approach, that Jan Phillips, the director of the College School, and Brenda returned to St. Louis to write the grant proposal described in the Prologue. The proposal was funded in July 1992. Once again, my family agreed to follow me, and we prepared to go to St. Louis instead of returning to our home in Vermont.

I was born in St. Louis and often had wished to return there to live as an adult; yet the opportunity had never presented itself. My parents still lived in the house I grew up in, and I had longed to be close to them in their elder years. It continues to be amazing to me that through traveling all the way to Italy on a year-long journey, I was offered the chance to return to my childhood home.

It was hard, nevertheless, to say good-bye to the community of friends we had found in Italy. It was also difficult to leave the context of community life lived in the piazzas, the public gardens, and the cafes of Reggio Emilia. We were not eager to trade outdoor market and small shop, fresh produce shopping for an impersonal, fluorescent-lit supermarket, or to exchange daily travel on a bicycle for dependency on a car. It would be a challenge for all of us to adjust to life in a major American city after that of a small Italian city, and before that, a small Vermont town. I knew that I would miss the teachers and children from the Diana and La Villetta Schools and the remarkable way of learning I had witnessed. I was afraid to leave.

I remember two exchanges with Italian educators before I left—one with Loris Malaguzzi and one with Sergio Spaggiari, the director of all the Reggio Emilia municipal preschools and infant/toddler centers. When I summoned the courage to tell Sergio that I wanted to find a way to stay in Reggio Emilia, he said, "Your work is just beginning. Your real work is in your country. You have to try. You have to see if you can apply what you've learned in your context, in your schools, with your teachers and children." I agreed with him, with a reluctance accompanied by a profound lack of confidence that I would find success.

Just before we left Reggio Emilia, I visited Loris Malaguzzi for the last time. I confessed that I was, indeed, worried that I would not be able to explain the complexity of what I had learned in his schools to an American audience, and that I did not know where to begin with the teachers I was to work with. He leaned forward on his desk, gesturing with his strong, wide hands, looked at me with one eyebrow raised and tried to reassure me, "It is not that hard, it can't be that hard—you always have to remember: Take one step forward and two steps back. Think about what you are doing. Don't rush forward without stopping." I told him that I would try to remember his advice, to which he exclaimed, "*In bocca al lupo!*" which means, "Good luck!" and is literally translated, "Jump in the wolf's mouth!"

BEGINNING AT THE COLLEGE SCHOOL

I remember arriving at the College School for my first day of work. It was just as my mother had described it—a big square, brick building tucked behind the intersection of two busy streets, behind a Chinese fast food restaurant, a quick-stop shop, across from a Pizza Hut. The approach was nothing like the one to the Diana School—across the park, under the cypress trees, past the outdoor cafes.

As I explained in the Prologue, the College School was once the laboratory school for Webster University and has always been based on an experiential, integrated, and thematic curriculum. The preschool would serve as my base and the eventual demonstration site for the Danforth-funded program through which I had been hired. I was at once excited by the prospect of this new opportunity and daunted by the enormity of the task. My year-long internship at the Diana and La Villetta Schools in Reggio Emilia, and my background in child development and arts education, were my preparation. I actually had never taught preschool children.

Driving around to the other side of the school, I was delighted to discover a lawn planted with fruit trees and shrubs opening out onto a park sloping down a graceful hill to a shaded grove of trees and a creek bed. I was early this first day and anxious about seeing the space in which I had agreed to work, sight unseen from Italy, as well as meeting the other teachers with whom I would work.

Before going inside the building, I wandered down the hill to sit against the trunk of one of the tall oaks to quietly observe the day and mark this new beginning with a wide-awake mind. This was an open space, with honeysuckle and bees, crows and squirrels—a small piece of wildness in the middle of a busy city. It could be a sanctuary for me, I thought. It could become a special place for children.

I walked up the hill at 9:00 and through the front doors of the school. I took in my new surroundings—freshly painted, warm gray walls, fabric-covered display boards, long corridors, an open area with couches and tables, and a friendly, bustling, informal atmosphere. I was soon greeted by Jan Phillips, and Joyce Devlin and Dorris Roberts, two of my co-teachers whom I had met when they visited Reggio Emilia the previous spring. We exchanged warm greetings as we walked down the hall toward the preschool classrooms.

At the end of the hall, we walked together through heavy, darkly stained wooden doors into a small, windowless room. From here, we peered into the predominantly dull beige and dark, cavernous space of the preschool. The rooms were empty and we could not enter them because the floors were being cleaned. I was in the front of the group, with Jan, Joyce, Dorris, and, by now, others behind me waiting to hear my reaction.

I remember feeling my heart sink. I thought, "How do I tell them that we can't do it here. We can't make something from nothing. How can we try to put an approach that is centered around light, order, and beauty into practice in a dark, ugly space?" I don't remember what I said, but my disappointment was not easy to hide. I thought I had been given an impossible task.

Nevertheless, the teachers and I began our work together that September—trying to make the best of the space, trying to understand the elements of the Reggio Approach in our context, and trying to learn from one another. Unlike me, they had taught preschool for many years. In a sense, they were waiting for me to teach them everything I had learned in Reggio Emilia and to take the lead. In another sense, it was difficult for them to let go of old ways and to experiment with new ones.

We began with three critical elements of the Reggio Approach. Together, we wanted to learn how to have conversations of quality with small groups of children; nurture and extend children's natural abilities in the many languages of the visual arts; and transform our classrooms from dark, dismal places into beautiful, inviting, light-filled, orderly spaces. Over the course of 4 years, we have learned a great deal through our work in all three of these challenging areas. In this chapter, I will discuss examples of our conversations with children and our work with children in three of the hundred languages—drawing, paint, and clay.

Although I will discuss them in sequence, our work in these areas developed simultaneously. As we were all feeling our way, one of my roles became that of "lead experimenter." My first experiments were in conversations with children.

CHILDREN AND SPOKEN LANGUAGE

I have always loved to listen to children's talk and to read their first written words about things that are fascinating and important to them. Their language is fresh, full of insight and metaphor, innocence and honesty. I have always felt I could learn from them—both to see the world with new eyes and to find words to describe what I see. In reflecting on these gifts of the child, I have searched to find their source.

The work of Jean Piaget, especially as interpreted by Margaret Donaldson (1979), has helped me to understand that the intuitive thought of the young child is based on immediate impressions that are rooted in the senses. This way of approaching the world allows the child to live outside the system of logic in which cause and effect and beginnings and endings often distance us, as adults, from the immediacy of our experience. This way of thinking gives the child the gift of language that is fresh and alive.

The writing of Heinz Werner (1948) suggests that children as well as artists and poets see the world physionomically. That is, they experience the way something "feels"—that sensation actually forms the world itself. For instance, to the child, a sharp-cornered object can be "cruel," a cup on its side can be "sad" or "tired," and a foggy day can be "whispery." This way of seeing gives the child the gift of metaphor and personification in perception and in language.

James Britton (1992), the prominent British linguist, begins a paper called "Language in Two Modes" with the following quote from Michael Oakeshott's book, *The Voice of Poetry in the Conversation of Mankind*: "Everybody's young days are a dream, a delightful insanity, a miraculous confusion of poetry and practical activity [when] we are moved not by the desire to communicate but by the delight of utterance" (p. 188).

Britton goes on to write that he believes that both poetic and practical language is found in varying proportions at all stages of development. He believes the desire to communicate leads toward "getting things done in the world." "The delight of utterance" (p. 189), on the other hand, represents language and talk as a pleasurable activity or talk *as play*. The inclination to play with the sounds and meanings of words gives the child both the freedom and the ability to invent rhymes and rhythms, syllables and songs.

Language links us to the world and to others. It is through speaking and listening to ideas in language that shared meanings are shaped and our singular perspectives are enriched. If children are encouraged to use language as they investigate and explore the world and as they reflect on their experience alongside their friends and supportive adults, they will learn to love language and to make it work for them as both "poetry and practical activity" (Britton, 1992).

Conversations with Children

Engaging in dialogue—talk with children about their ideas about something of importance—is a key component of the work in the Reggio Emilia preschools. The group of children can be large (the whole class), medium (around 10 to 15), or small (around three to six). Teachers also have conversations with pairs of children or one child at a time. The idea every time is to explore the children's ideas.

The teacher's role is to ask good, open-ended questions that stimulate children's thinking and provoke discussion—to facilitate, orchestrate, and gently guide so that the conversation does not stray too far from the subject, so that every child has a chance to participate, and so that children consider the matter at hand with all their attention and interest. In these conversations the teacher does not fish for right answers or impart information. This is clearly a departure from the traditional idea of the teacher's role.

Lev Vygotsky, the noteworthy Russian linguist, is one of the theorists who have influenced the development and practice of the small-group conversation in the Reggio Emilia preschools. In her book, *Apprenticeship in Thinking*, Barbara Rogoff (1990) writes that according to Vygotsky's theory, children's participation in communicative processes is the foundation on which they build their understanding.

> As children listen to the views and understanding of others and stretch their concepts to find a common ground; as they collaborate and argue with others, consider new alternatives, and recast their ideas to communicate or to convince, they advance their ideas in the process of participation. It is a matter of social engagement that leaves the individual changed. (pp. 195–196)

The motivation for placing these conversations at the center of the curriculum is to enable children to develop their critical and creative thinking ability to its fullest; to promote cooperation, interaction, and negotiation among children; and to celebrate children's natural curiosity and wonder about the world and how it works (Fyfe & Cadwell, 1993). It is also a way of taking time together, teacher and child, to focus on important aspects of life and living; to examine an experience, an object, or an idea closely; and to wonder and search together.

Carlina Rinaldi, the pedagogical director of the preschools in Reggio Emilia, offers specific advice on this subject.

> Children are searching for the real meaning of life. We believe in their possibilities to grow. That is why we do not hurry to give them answers; instead we invite them to think about where the answers might lie. The challenge is to listen. When your child asks, ''Why is there a moon?'' don't reply with a scientific answer. Ask him, ''What do you think?'' He will understand that you are telling him, ''You have your own mind and your own interpretation and your ideas are important to me.'' Then you and he can look for the answers, sharing the wonder, curiosity, pain—everything. It is not the answers that are important, it is the process—that you and he search together. (quoted in McLaughlin, 1995, p. 65)

In his book *The Uses of Enchantment*, Bruno Bettelheim (1977) offers further rationale for refraining from giving children quick and easy scientifically ''correct'' answers to their questions. He warns:

> Realistic explanations are usually incomprehensible to children because they lack the abstract understanding required to make sense of them. While giving scientifically correct answers makes adults think they have clarified things for the child, such explanations leave the young child confused, overpowered, and intellectually defeated. . . . Even as the child accepts such an answer, he comes to doubt that he has asked the right question. (pp. 47–48)

My only experience in the art of having conversations with small groups of preschool children had been in Italy and, therefore, with Italian children. I was eager to try my hand in my native language. I had followed many different conversations with 3-, 4-, and 5-year-old children and their teachers at the Diana and La Villetta schools and had led several conversations toward the end of the year at the Diana School. I thought I understood the basics.

I began by taking a small group of five or six 4-year-old children out of the classroom to converse about a variety of subjects. My first attempts were experiments. The children and I had some successes and some failures. We conversed about the classroom pet, Princess, a guinea pig; and about a huge bouquet of sunflowers brought in by a parent. I found my way, learning more and more about appropriate questions, how to best compose a group that might think and work well together, how to pace a conversation, how to record it, and how to stay out of it when necessary.

My first remarkable conversation with children was about leaves and the changing seasons. It is still one of my favorites and one that convinced me very early on that American children are every bit as bright and capable as Italian children! This conversation was based on rich experiences playing in the falling autumn leaves, noticing all the changes happening around them as fall progressed, and wondering together about these phenomena. I think it is as rich as it is because we had dedicated so much time to exploring the hillside and the oak trees that grew just outside our school. The hillside was becoming our outdoor classroom and a special place for me and the children, just as I had anticipated on the first day I came to the College School. This conversation with seven 4-year-old children and myself took place on October 21, 1992, around a basket of leaves that we had collected outside (see Figure 4.1).

Louise: What do you see?

Michael: This part is white and this is red (*turning the leaf over*). I wonder why? That must be the skin (*pointing to the underside*). This must be the body (*pointing to the top*). The sticks, the little things going out in the leaf, must be bones!

Katie: You can see parts of bones on mine, too. See the things pointing out. The red is the body. Those little stubs must be the bones.

David: I found the spine!

Katie: I found the spine, too.

Meredith: I know that. Everybody has a spine.

David: It's straight (*feeling his spine*). I can feel the bumps of it.

Meredith: It's like little hills. It goes up and down.

David: Don't break it [the spine], then you can't move at all.

Katie: This part is like the leg (*pointing to the stem*).

Louise: Does the leaf walk?

Figure 4.1. Wondering About Leaves Together

Michael: No, it flies! I guess its flying is its walking.

Katie: And it jumps and skips.

Louise: Why do you think the leaves fall?

Devyn: Because at the end of fall they kind of curl up to sleep, because they are tired.

David: Because they are dead.

Louise: When they fall off the branches, are they dead?

Devyn: They are asleep, when they fall. They curl up so they don't get cold. The leaves fall down because they are asleep. They die. It's too cold for them to live.

David: But the tree doesn't die. Maybe it does, but not for a very long time.

Louise: How could the leaves ever turn these colors?

Meredith: They turn that way, 'cause I know why. Magic comes when it's fall. It turns the leaves to red and all colors. It gets very, very cold.

Michael: It's like Terminator! The bad guy changed to different things, like the leaves, so nobody knows who he is. It's like putting on Halloween costumes. Maybe somebody has the power to change the leaves.

Elysia: The wind has the magic power. It makes the leaves change.

Michael: I think the more the wind blows, the more the magic goes into the leaves and changes them.

Dan: 'Cause somebody gots magic.

Katie: I know who does it; the wind and the rain and the clouds and the sun. God does it!

Michael: I knew something was going on.

"Reading" a Conversation

One of the things I learned from the teachers in Reggio Emilia was just how important it is to "read" and understand a dialogue like this. This is a seemingly casual conversation; yet, it has pushed the children to draw on their experience, to hypothesize, to wonder, and to venture forth into new territory together.

If we read the conversation carefully, what knowledge can we say these children have? What examples can we find in this conversation of their use of intuition, conjecture, logical and creative thinking? When have they made analogies and used metaphors to communicate their ideas? How has listening to the ideas of their classmates challenged them, informed them, and offered them a new way of viewing the problem? What can we, as adults, learn from them about the way they look at and think about leaves? What might we do next with these children? Could we include a larger group with whom we could share these initial ideas to support further learning?

Because of the opportunity to think about these ideas together, this group of children has discovered and expressed a whole network of ideas about leaves. Through observing carefully and feeling both sides of the leaf, Michael has discovered that leaves have an internal structure that reminds him of bones. This excites David to name the leaf "spine," which in turn sparks the children to focus for a minute on their own spines and what they know about them. Following Katie's analogy of the stem to a leg, Michael makes another movement analogy, "Its flying is its walking." Katie then extends the vision, imagining a leaf flying in the wind saying that the leaf "jumps and skips." Noticing the similarity of skeletal forms in animal and plant life is a big idea and an extraordinary relationship to make. All the children and their teacher are excited and amazed at the discovery. Remembering and describing the way a leaf moves through the air as "flying, jumping, and skipping" relates to the way the children move, or wish they could, and offers all of us a delightful, metaphorical way to think about leaves in the wind.

When asked why she thinks the leaves fall, Devyn identifies with them saying she thinks they are tired from the summer and want to go to sleep. David adds a note of realism, reminding her bluntly that the leaves are not asleep, but dead. Devyn listens and accepts what David says, yet she wants the death to be soft and gentle. She says, "They are asleep, when they fall." She thinks maybe it is not too bad a fate for them because they are curled up to keep warm. She then returns to her first idea, adding that the *reason* the leaves fall is *because* they have fallen asleep. She finishes, reluctantly explaining, "They die. It's too cold for them to live."

This exchange reminds me of the one in Reggio Emilia toward the end of the Tree Project about the death of the apple blossoms. The girls felt sad at the death of the blossoms, saying the parent flower would never see its child, the fruit. They added that the death of a blossom is light and not as heavy as a human death, perhaps making the phenomenon more acceptable. Similarly, the death of the leaves is more bearable to Devyn if they are asleep. In each case, there is an intimate identification with the plant world and, through leaves, an understanding of the life cycle.

Through his studies of children, Jean Piaget showed that this animistic way of viewing the world lasts throughout childhood. The young child believes that even inanimate objects are inhabited by spirits very much like people, so they feel and act like people (Bettelheim, 1977). If we accept this way in which children see the world as their own special intelligence instead of thinking it is cute and/or incorrect, we have much to learn from the children we listen to.

In this conversation, we can appreciate the intimacy and empathy that these children feel and express for the plant world. In part, they feel this kind of empathy because they attribute human feelings to the leaves. This practice is not limited to young children, however. St. Francis, the patron saint of Italy and one of the first recorded Italian poets, wrote "The Canticle of Brother Sun" in the twelfth century (Brady, 1988). In this hymn of thanksgiving, he addressed the elements of the earth by name, personifying and praising each of them. Many other poets and artists have done the same throughout history. All cultures pass down stories and fairy tales that bring the natural world to life. This is a way for children and adults to reach out to the natural world and at the same time to turn inside the world of dreams in which rocks are able to speak and flowers to sing.

Even though Piaget would describe these children's ideas as egocentric because they identify with the leaves' movement and structure through their own bodies, in many ways the sentiments seem to be the opposite of the true meaning of the word *egocentric*. To identify with the other, to imagine what life must be like for another being, and to see the interconnected nature of all living things—these are among the sentiments and values that we wish to encourage in children and in adults. These sentiments and values are at the root of establishing a deep connection to the natural world and a strong sense of place.

I believe that real and lasting relationships emerge from this kind of exploration together—relationships that establish ties to the leaves, to the trees, to the wind, to each other, to the joy of having and sharing wonderful ideas (Duckworth, 1995), and, as Carlina says, to the pleasure and pain of the search together.

In considering both the wonder and possible cause of the leaves' change to vibrant colors, Meredith suggests that magic comes when it gets very, very cold. Michael jumps to a striking metaphor, "It's like Terminator!" who, he explains, magically changes his form so as to disguise himself. Michael takes his metaphor further. "It's like putting on Halloween costumes," he says, and then adds that maybe Terminator or some other superhero has special powers to change the leaves!

The children's ideas are tumbling out, following one another, weaving together, creating fantastic possibilities. They are all intensely engaged. Elysia whispers, "The wind has the magic power. It makes the leaves change." After a pause, Michael offers a quantitative addition to Elysia's hypothesis, saying that the more wind blows, the more the magic enters the leaves and changes their color. Dan is enthralled. He has been fascinated and quiet. He now adds his assertion, "'Cause somebody gots magic."

Katie says she knows who changes the leaves! No more guesswork. No more hocus pocus. She says that the wind and the rain and the clouds and the sun and God are responsible. To me, Katie is intuitively pulling this remarkable conversation together. There *is* magic in the changing leaves. Even to those of us who might think we understand the scientific reasons behind this phenomenon, it is a miracle if we are wide enough awake to see it. And the wind and the rain that come in the fall, the changing axis of the earth pulling away from the sun, all these things do cause the change in seasons, which in the end transforms the leaves. Is it magic? Is there a logical explanation? Is it caused by the elements of earth, water, and sun? Is it God's doing? These children think all these perspectives are true. When Michael ends with a statement as full of awe as of new understanding, "I knew something was going on," he speaks for all of us.

Learning How to Listen to and Talk with Children

The teachers in Reggio Emilia find the time in a regularly scheduled meeting or perhaps during the day to review an important conversation together. In their meeting they might also analyze a teacher's participation. Were the questions good ones? Did the teacher do a good job facilitating the conversation? What about the timing of the questions? Was she or he supporting the children enough? Did every child participate? Why or why not? Did the teacher intervene too much or too little. In this way, with the critical support of their colleagues, the teachers become better and better facilitators of this kind of inquiry.

The educators in Reggio Emilia prepare for conversations. They devote enough time and full attention to the children and their ideas in a quiet space, giving children and teachers the respect they need. Then, with their colleagues they study the transcripts of the recorded conversations and use them as the core of their ongoing work with children. This is a style of working for them.

It is not a style of working for educators in the United States. This kind of practice poses many challenges. I did not find immediate support or excitement on the part of teachers to try this approach. In my self-designated role as lead experimenter at the College School, I tried to entice other teachers to experiment so that we could begin to understand and incorporate this fundamental aspect of the Reggio Approach into our work with children. It seemed an exciting opportunity to me, and I was surprised to meet with resistance and resentment.

Obstacles We Encountered

With hindsight, after 4 years of work at the College School and the other schools in our network, we all have a better understanding of the difficulties that we faced and still face. It might be useful to review some of the obstacles we have encountered in bringing quality conversations and discussions with children into our curriculum planning and daily practice.

The first is the issue of fairness and equity for teachers and children (Fyfe, 1994). Is it fair to give a small group of children that much attention? What happens to the other children? Don't they feel left out? Is it fair for one teacher to have the luxury of focusing on a small group of children for 45 minutes or more? Isn't she or he supposed to be responsible for all the children? If there is no co-teacher, how would this ever be possible? If there is, is it fair to leave the co-teacher with the majority of the children?

We have learned through experience that we must plan in advance and agree how we will support each other and the children while one of us works with a small group and the others are with the larger group. We have begun to ask ourselves instead, Is it fair to deny children these rich opportunities to learn from each other and with a teacher in a small-group setting? We know that all children deserve this kind of attention and that over time we can give it to them (Cadwell & Fyfe, 1997).

A second challenge is noise. It is impossible to have a quality conversation if children and teachers are distracted by the noise of a busy classroom and constant distractions of other children who interrupt. In order to think, to listen, and to discuss, children and teachers need separate, quiet spaces. These are hard to come by in early childhood settings.

With the support of the College School director and a group of parents, we have been able to raise the funds to create the private spaces necessary for this kind of focused attention to a small group. This will be discussed in more detail in Chapter 5. In addition to these spaces, we also use temporarily unoccupied rooms or go outside.

A third consideration is expectation. Traditionally, most teachers do not expect young children to sit in a small group for half an hour or more to discuss ideas and theories about the workings of the world. Teachers might think this is too much to expect of preschool children. Maybe it is even harmful to them to expect them to sit and think when they might rather play with manipulatives, blocks, or dress-ups.

Most of us who have begun to practice small-group conversations have been amazed at young children's ability to engage in rich and long conversations. Their abilities and interest seem to depend on us. As we teachers become more skilled in providing the best conditions for high-quality experiences and conversations, the children's capacity to focus and to articulate their ideas grows. With our perception of them as capable, strong, and prepared as opposed to fidgety and incapable, their contributions increase and their words and ideas flow.

A fourth barrier is rationale. Why do this? What value is there for children? What value for teachers? What do children and teachers learn from this kind of activity? How do you make use of this kind of information? Where do you go with it? How does it fit in with the rest of the curriculum? What happens to the skills and information teachers are supposed to teach if they are spending so much time listening to children's ideas?

This question is a central one for those of us who create curriculum. Preplanned curriculum assumes that we know what children need to learn, what they will be able to learn, and how they will best learn. Emergent curriculum requires teachers to listen to children's ideas and interests and to connect their curriculum goals with those of the children in responsive and creative ways (Cadwell & Fyfe, 1997).

A fifth deterent to facilitating small-group conversations is lack of skill. It takes skill and practice to be able to lead a productive conversation with young children. Teachers need to have the courage to risk failures in order to try. However, once teachers begin to organize the time to listen to children and to think about the ways in which they seek to make sense of the world, the teachers will be reluctant to talk and "teach" so much of the time. Most often, they will find ways to improve their new practice of listening. Often, the support of a group helps teachers gain necessary skills. Sometimes, a teacher who is comfortable with the process can model for the rest of the group.

A sixth difficulty is recording. How do you record what the children say? It is possible to take notes, but it is very hard to lead a conversation and take notes at the same time; however, this is one way to begin. Children often will be impressed that their teacher is interested enough in their ideas to want to write them down and remember them. If available, an aid or parent volunteer can take notes. However, using a tape recorder is the best way to record a conversation. Finding the time to transcribe the tape seems to become easier after teachers understand the real value of conversations.

A seventh challenge is the review, analysis, and planning, with a group of colleagues, for further use of the information gained. This, again, takes time, commitment, organization, and skill. It is a necessary piece of the puzzle of the place of conversations in the early childhood curriculum. Otherwise, the conversations are left behind, without connection or relationship to the life of the children and teachers in the school. They become isolated events rather than critical connectors and resources for children and teachers.

These are complicated issues. It is clear that what seemed a relatively simple, new way to work with young children turned out to require teachers to rethink and change their assumptions about and expectations of children, their way of organizing their time and their style of working, and their way of developing curriculum and planning their days and activities (Fyfe, 1994). It required them to develop new skills and take risks, to give extra time, to collaborate, and to critique each other. None of these changes is simple. After 4 years, we are still struggling with some aspects of all of them, even though we have made progress together and we are committed to finding solutions. Many of the difficulties center around time and organization. As we find better ways to organize and share our work, we are able to meet the challenges of this way of working together with children.

Some Suggestions for Good Conversations

We have all learned many things over the past 4 years of having conversations with children. Among the things that we have learned through trial and error are the following tenets for having good conversations:

1. Think about appropriate questions beforehand. Try to brainstorm with colleagues first. Think about what kinds of questions would stimulate children's curiosity, provoke and challenge them to wonder and hypothesize, invent and compare.
2. Arrange to have the conversation in a quiet place where neither you nor the children will be distracted.
3. Choose a group that you feel will benefit from being together and that will work well together for any number of reasons. For example, the combination of interested children with less interested children, verbal with not so verbal, can work. Pay as careful attention to the group composition as the situation allows. Some opportunities will be more spontaneous than others. A group of five seems to be an ideal small-group number.
4. Know how you will record. Although it is difficult, some people can write quickly and keep up with the flow of the conversation. If you tape record, be committed to listening and transcribing the important parts of the tape as soon as you can. If another teacher can be with you, one can lead, one can write.
5. Let children know right away that you have no interest in quizzing them and that you don't know all the answers; that instead you want to wonder and search with them and that you are interested in big ideas and you know they are, too.
6. Communicate through your tone of voice your wonder, your belief in the children's capabilities to think creatively and critically, your excitement at this opportunity to talk together about important ideas.
7. Use the questions you have prepared as possibilities. Remain open to the flow of the conversation. It may go in interesting directions you had not anticipated. On the other hand, guide the conversation back to the main subject if it strays too far off.
8. Be the children's memory. Every once in a while, summarize for them what has been said, using names of children if possible. This will help them realize you are listening carefully and that their ideas are going on record. It also will help them look backward to what has been said and move forward with new ideas.
9. Stay in the background as much as possible when the children begin to talk to each other, debate, and ask each other questions. This way the conversation begins to belong to them, they become more invested in it, and they begin to learn to discuss among themselves without intervention.
10. Enjoy the conversation! Laugh together. Be amazed at their perspectives. Share some of yours.

11. Use the conversation. Share some of the things that were said, that day or the next, with the whole group of children. Use the conversation again with the same group or a different group. Ask children to expand on their ideas, critique their ideas, draw their ideas, paint or sculpt their ideas—translate and transform them into different languages. Analyze the children's ideas with your colleagues to decide whether to ask more questions, suggest further exploration and experience, and/or work with drawing or sculptural materials.

12. Recognize that children and adults need time and experience with this way of being together. Most children need time to understand what this is all about—that you really are serious about wanting them to think and tell you and the other children what they think, feel, and wonder about and that you have high expectations of them.

13. Be brave enough to discuss the conversations you conduct with children with other adults. It will help you gain skill and confidence.

In their book, *The Language of Primary School Children*, Connie and Harold Rosen (1974) give practical examples of rich language development in a social context. To illustrate the role of the adult in this process, they describe a particular teacher's approach.

> [She] is relaxed enough to *listen* with care and to appreciate exactly what children are able to express, and the subtle new advances which they make. She always directs their attention back to the essence of their own lives [and invites them] to turn their own language upon this world. . . . At the same time she knows that she is the initiator at the outset, . . . if the children are to take over, it is because she has opened up the possibilities and established the tone. (p. 228)

This kind of model teaching gives full credence to the intelligence and imagination of young children. It challenges them, alongside their peers, to reach for their own language to describe their world and their experience. It encourages them to play with spoken language "moved by the delight in utterance" and at the same time to use language to wonder about, examine, order, and communicate what they understand.

CHILDREN AND MATERIALS

Another area in which I took the role as lead experimenter was in the graphic and sculptural languages of the visual arts. Before interning in the Reggio Emilia preschools, I had taught as an art teacher at the elementary level for 7 years and studied, from a developmental perspective, children's growth through making symbols. Although I had studied the work of young children and taught kindergarten for many years, my only previous training with preschool children and art materials outside of Italy occurred during a week of observation of classes for young children and their parents taught by Muriel Silberstein at the Metropolitan Museum of Art in New York City. There, children and parents, each at their own level, discovered the joy and expressive power of drawing materials, paint, clay, and collage. I was inspired to experiment with her ideas with my two young sons and then to offer a similar class based on her approach.

During these experiences with very young children, I saw for myself what Rhoda Kellogg (Kellogg & O'Dell, 1967) makes clear—that all children, no matter where they live in the world, have a need and find a way to draw. Making marks and visual symbols is as natural and as necessary to children as making sounds and speaking. Kellogg demonstrates that all children follow predictable patterns in developing a repertoire of lines and forms.

At about the age of 2, all children begin to make marks, on paper if it is given to them, but also in the dirt, in the sand, with sticks, and with their fingers. Around the age of 3, children usually begin to outline shapes. They draw circles and ovals, squares and rectangles, triangles and crosses. Between the ages of 4 and 5, with a knowledge of these basic patterns, shapes, and designs, children discover that their structured designs can resemble objects in the world (Kellogg & O'Dell, 1967).

These early approaches to drawing can be seen in children's encounters with other materials, like clay, paper sculpture, collage, and paint. As young children act on these materials and move them around in space, gradually they discover that they can give them intentional form and shape.

Viktor Lowenfeld (1964) calls this later stage of growth in making visual symbols (from about ages 4 to 7) the *preschematic* stage. At this age, children begin to establish relationships with objects and experiences in the world through their efforts to represent them.

Many experts seem to agree that the child at this stage is intent on establishing relationships (Burton, 1991; Lowenfeld, 1964; Smith, Fucigna, Kennedy, & Lord, 1993; Vecchi, 1993). In a paper entitled "Some Basic Considerations About 'Basic Art,'" Judith Burton (1991) discusses the importance of developing relationships of increasing complexity with materials and with the world of our experience.

> The arts are important because in the act of making we actually *engage* with the world of our experience while at the same time we are invited to deeper reflection of that world as our ideas and responses become visual realities: as paintings and drawings emerge from materials. (pp. 36–39)

My experience in Reggio Emilia convinced me that all children have the right to work and play with a wide range of the highest-quality materials in the highest-quality settings in their daily life in school. It is in this way that children are able to build rich and complex relationships with the world, which will grow and evolve over time.

Of all the "hundred languages" I knew and learned more about in Reggio Emilia, I felt the most affinity with drawing pens and pencils, tempera paint, and clay. These are the materials that I loved and used most with children during my years as an art teacher, and the materials I considered and others recommended as the most basic for the young child (Burton, 1980; Lowenfeld, 1964). We began by introducing these materials at the College School.

During my first year, we also introduced varieties of collage materials, high-quality colored pencils, markers, oil pastels, and watercolors, along with a light table. Since then, we, alongside the children, have learned more about the possibilities of paper and wire sculpture and weaving. In the next sections, I will describe how we introduced the first three materials—drawing media, tempera paint, and clay, and tell some of the stories that emerged out of the interaction between the children and the materials.

Taking Ideas About Leaves into Graphic Form

During our investigation of leaves, we mixed autumn colors we had noticed outside from quarts of a wide range of tempera colors. Many children had the opportunity to paint at the easel and to use these colors. I wanted to offer the children the chance to make stronger connections with their experience in the midst of this brilliant season through autumn hues in painting. (This approach will be discussed in detail in the section on tempera paint.)

At the same time, graphic materials such as varieties of soft to hard lead pencils, black fine-line markers, good-quality thick markers, and high-quality, soft lead, colored pencils, as well as a variety of white and muted tones of paper in different sizes, were available to the children to use daily for drawing. I was accustomed to using black drawing pens with children. I had used them as a basic material ever since I spent a year as an intern in England, where children used them frequently for drawing and writing. They produce a quality of line that is fluid yet strong, fine yet definite. Even the very young child can discover the joy of making a precise line.

However, they were new to the preschool teachers in St. Louis. Some said they had always been told that it was harmful for children to make such small drawings because they didn't yet have the necessary fine motor control. We all noticed that the preschool children at the College School seemed to like the pens and to use them with ease and control.

The teachers also seemed skeptical about the idea of suggesting that children draw "from life" or from looking at something specific. Again, they were concerned that this request was asking too much of young children. I thought of Vea, who helped me understand that she didn't want to rush children along, only to offer them the possibility of making relationships between their marks and their experience. If they were ready, they would make the connections, which would be *their* connections. If they were not ready, they wouldn't.

After discussing the idea with my colleagues, one day I put a variety of leaves we had collected outside on a table with several types of black drawing pens. At the morning meeting I asked if a group of children might like to draw the leaves. All but two children in the class had already been representing themselves in self-portraits. Most of the children had used a combination of large circles, small circles, lines, and dots to represent themselves, other people, and other things. Some of them had done quite sophisticated and detailed representational drawings. I thought that they might be ready to use these same elements to represent the leaves. As a way of illustrating the range of responses and some of the connections these children were able to make, I will describe four different children's approaches to drawing the leaves.

David

Among several others, Elysia and David, who had been part of the conversation on leaves, chose to draw that morning. David chose a thick, black marker and, after considering the leaves briefly, drew four roundish-oval shapes with a line attached for a stem. He then drew horizontal stripes across each of the four shapes to represent the leaf bones. He added two small ovals and then wrote his name in three letters (see Figure 4.2). David used his schema for a contained shape, a circle, to draw the leaf. He did not distinguish between the different kinds of leaves or address the variations or curvy lines that defined some of the leaves. He did include the "bones" we had discovered, but not the spine. He

FIGURE 4.2. David's Drawing

stayed at the table about 15 minutes. He was enthusiastic and confident about his drawing.

Elysia

Elysia chose a fine-line marker and two different leaves from the basket, an oak and a beech. She began with the elegant oak. She drew the spine and then the lobes in half circles that met at the spine. She enjoyed these petticoat-like, lacy lines that she made, so she drew another baby oak leaf for fun. She then drew the simpler form of the beech, defining it with two curved lines that met on each end. At one point, she stopped to examine the leaf more closely and began to try to draw the tiny zig-zag lines on the edge of the leaf, but it proved too laborious, so she stopped. She then drew the leaf spine and horizontal lines, "bones," on one side of the spine. Examining the leaf again, she noticed that the "bones" actually were slanted from the spine to the edge, so she tried another way of drawing them. She invented a zig-zaggy line halfway through the other side of the beech leaf. She finished by writing her name (see Figure 4.3). She stayed at the table about 40 minutes.

Michael and Jessica

Among other children, I wanted to encourage Michael, who had been such a strong leader in our leaf conversation, to paint or draw the leaves. Early in the year, Michael's mother had told us that he hated "art" and that he would not participate in it. In fact, he was very reluctant to draw or paint. I decided to start by inviting him to paint because it would be the more free and, perhaps, seductive medium.

I suggested he might want to enjoy the colors and the lines, patches of color or designs he could make with them. I added that he might want to paint some of his ideas like the "leaf bones," or the leaves "flying, jumping, and skipping," or himself in the leaves. I said the choice was up to him. I had learned this way of making suggestions, which leaves the content and direction of the work up to the child, from a curriculum by Judy Burton and Nancy Smith (1978). The approach offers children the idea that their work does not need to be representative, but that it can be. The choice is theirs. They are free and supported in making the marks they can and need to make, and in giving them their own significance. I hoped the colors and Michael's strong ideas and feelings about the leaves would entice him to paint that day. However, they did not.

Later that week, I decided to see if Michael would sit at a table next to Jessica and try some leaf drawings (see Figure 4.4). We brought over the basket of leaves we had collected, and together we picked out a jar of black drawing pens and a jar of soft drawing pencils from the studio shelves.

Jessica was very comfortable with drawing. She drew spontaneously, eagerly, and often. I hoped that her enthusiasm and confidence would encourage Michael. Michael told Jessica and me that he couldn't draw a leaf. I said I was certain that he could. Jessica agreed and began to draw with a medium-point black marker. Michael watched her look at the leaf and begin to make lines go in and out to define the lobes of the leaf. He saw that Jessica had invented a way to use the pen that would match the curves of the oak leaf. He decided to try. He

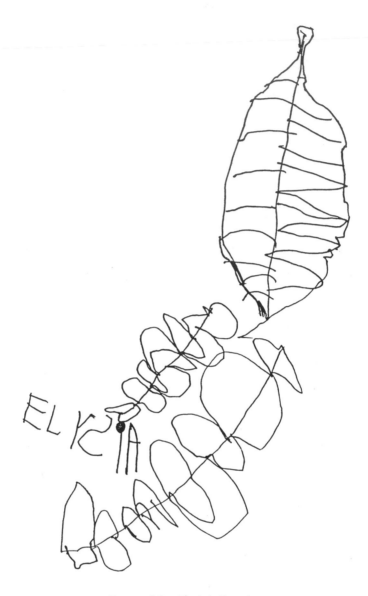

FIGURE 4.3. Elysia's Drawing

looked carefully at the oak leaf he held in his hand. Slowly and tentatively, he followed the curly edges of the leaf with his eye and his pen. He began to draw. When he finished, he was thrilled with his results. He wanted to paint the "leaf body" with watercolor.

The next week, Michael chose a pencil, and next to his leaf body drawing he drew lightly a central line to represent the spine, with horizontal lines coming off each side for the bones. These pencil lines represented the leaf skeleton, which is left as the leaf begins to decompose. By this time, because we had gone farther with our conversations and investigations of the fate of the falling leaves, Michael had examined many leaf skeletons. He had learned about their structure and their lightness. He represented his knowledge and feeling for the leaf as it moves from life to death through using three different media—strong, black pen, soft pencil, and watercolors—in what were among his first representative drawings (see Figure 4.5). Later in the year, Michael began to enjoy the freedom of painting at the easel and working on murals alongside his friends.

Jessica's drawing has a different quality. She is skilled in representing herself. She has a strong sense of design and she is confident in drawing "from life." Here, she has used a black fine-line marker to draw the oak leaf, yet she has added her fanciful swirls and curlicues, enamored with the play and freedom of lines. She has taken the lines into a drawing of herself in the middle of the leaves, joyfully participating beside them in the autumn season (see Figure 4.6). Through line she has graphically represented her knowledge of leaf form and shape, her love of decorative twirls and spirals, and the joy of her participation in the midst of the experience of noticing and learning.

Tempera Paint Stories: Snow Experiences

Tempera paint is found in virtually every classroom for young children in this country and in many other countries. It is generally agreed that it is an important medium for young children. Because of its fluidity and saturated color, it has long been considered the most expressive art medium (Lowenfeld, 1964). The way tempera paint is presented to and used by children, however, varies dramatically.

FIGURE 4.4. Michael Drawing His Leaf

FIGURE 4.5.   Michael's Drawing

I had learned and always used a way of presenting primary colors and white and black tempera to kindergarten and primary children in small containers on individual trays with a jar of water and a sponge to wipe their brushes (Burton & Smith, 1978; Smith et al., 1993). This approach seemed to make good sense. Accompanied by some instruction in how to use it, the system encouraged children to mix new colors, allowed them to work on a horizontal surface so they did not have to concern themselves with drips, and enabled them to learn to rinse and wipe their brush between colors.

I had discovered, however, that although children always enjoyed the fluidity of the paint and the new colors that they invented, the colors they were able to mix often were not particularly pleasing. For some reason, the average commercial primaries did not mix beautiful new secondary colors; instead blue and yellow made an army green, and red and blue made a deep, brownish plum.

When I saw even very young children in Reggio Emilia painting with three or four gradations of yellows, pinks, blues, and greens, on easels outside in the spring air, or 4-year-olds investigating and then painting the variations of violets and greens in the wisteria blooming on the trellis outside their school, I felt that surely even those of us with much experience and background could learn a great deal from this way of introducing young children to paint. When I queried Vea Vecchi about the rationale behind the wide choice of color, she told me:

> The world is full of many gradations of color. We give the children the primary colors and white and black. In addition, we give them several gradations of all the colors. We believe this offers them more possibilities. When they start with these gradations, they mix even more.

The expectation was not that the children would paint in a sophisticated way beyond their reach, only that they might begin to make more relationships—the possibility was open to them. As Vea explained to me, they might be ready to make the connection between the sky and the colors they chose and marks they made, or they might not be. They might take the colors and the painting experience in a completely different fanciful or personal direction. They might simply enjoy the colors as they appeared on the paper. I was eager to try this approach with American children.

FIGURE 4.6. Jessica's Drawing

My first year in the College School preschool, I began by mixing several tones of each color from primary and secondary colors and white. We kept the paint in clear jars so the colors could be seen. We kept the jars on a rolling cart, which could be moved from the sink to the easels and back again. We offered several kinds of brushes—some fat and sturdy, some softer and not so fat, some with short handles, some with long handles. With our help, the children learned to wash and care for the brushes and put the lids on the paint jars at the end of the day.

Painting was offered as a possible choice for children at several times during the day, with little adult suggestion as to subject. Many children at the College School seemed attracted to the luscious choice of colors. There were two easels next to each other and often children showed great interest in what their classmates next to them were painting. I saw children approach the paint and the paper in many different ways—some made linear, circular line paintings, others applied patches of paint laid down side by side, and still others painted great layers and mixtures of colors. Some painted with great energy and quick movements, while others painted in a calculated, methodical way. Some made a few tentative marks in a short time, while others worked fully absorbed most of the morning. Most of the time, some kind of story emerged as the painting took shape on the page.

I would like to give two examples of tempera paint stories that grew out of wintertime explorations of our "outdoor classroom"—the hillside and glade across the lane and down the hill from the school. The first is about a walk outside on a snowy day with a group of five boys and girls and a collective mural that became a memory of their discoveries in the snow. The second is a story of two boys as they discovered qualities of color and paint through a rich exchange of observations and imaginative ideas while painting together at the easel.

Taking a Walk, Making a Mural

It had been cold and snowy for a week or more, and all of the children and teachers had played outside enjoying the white world. One morning, we invited several children from both classes to explore farther afield. I remembered a day in Reggio Emilia when I went outside with three 5-year-old girls to discover what the trees must feel like under the snow. Vea had suggested that we begin by talking together inside about what we thought we might discover outside. This seems to be a way of heightening curiosity and expectation for children and adults. Thus, I chose to begin our snowy day expedition on January 23, 1995, with a conversation indoors among 3-year-old Kelly, Alexandra, and Olivia, and 4-year-old Robert and Jodie.

Louise: What do you think we'll find when we go outside?
Kelly: Treasures; probably diamonds!
Robert: It will be cold. Maybe we'll find a bear cave.
Jodie: There's snow outside.
Olivia: There will be food.
Louise: Like berries for the birds?
Robert: Are we going down to the woods? I like it down there.
Louise: Would you like that?

Olivia: Yeah. Can we go?

Louise: Do you think there will be snow on the trees?

Kelly: I don't know. I don't think so.

(*This part of the conversation occurred outside.*)

Kelly: There is snow on the bushes! And, you can see smoke coming from your mouth.

Jodie: Look at the tree. There are red berries and corn. Are they for the birds? Can we eat them?

Olivia: (*Jumping*) Look at what I can make in the snow!

Louise: Are you making footprints?

Robert: Me too. Look at my prints.

Louise: Hey, what's this? (*pointing to cracks in the snow*)

Kelly: They are snowy lines walking down the hill!

Louise: What do you hear when we walk?

Jodie: Scrunch, scrunch, scrunch.

Kelly: It crunches.

Robert: Hey, look at this; a miracle! It's ice.

(*All the children bend down to see closely.*)

Olivia: The snow on top is like sugar.

(*Down in the glade, the children find sticks and begin to draw in the snow.*)

Louise: Look, you're drawing lines in the snow.

(*Alexandra draws a circle with lines crossing in it.*)

Kelly: Look, I found more tracks.

Louise: What do you think they are?

Olivia: I think they are a bird's.

Louise: Alexandra, it looks a little like the drawing you were making with the stick.

(*Several children begin to make tracks of lines in the snow. They all have drawing sticks now.*)

Robert: Look, I found treasure! Here's another one! (*a cement block among frosted, snowy ivy*)

Jodie: And, look, more tracks!

Louise: What are those?

Robert: Maybe a kitty. Kitty tracks.

Louise: My toes and fingers are getting frozen. Shall we go in? Look, the sun is coming out!

Kelly: It's so sparkly. It is like diamonds [see Figure 4.7].

What wonderful things and ideas to bring back from our snowy day travels—treasures, diamonds, a bear cave, snow like sugar, breath like smoke, prints in the snow, the fun of drawings with sticks. For the children, it has been a great adventure into the wild world. Bringing back little pieces of ice and the drawing sticks along with their memories was an important part of the journey. It reminds me of what Scott Russell Sanders (1995) remembers of his childhood

FIGURE 4.7. A Snowy Day Walk

in his essay "News of the Wild." He tells us that whenever he returned home from a journey, even as short as a walk around the backyard, his father would ask, "What did you find?"

> And I would show him a fossil or a feather, tell him how the sun lit up the leaves of the hickory, how a skunk looked me over; I would recall for him the tastes of elderberries or the rush of wind in the white pines or the crunch of locust shells underfoot. Only in that sharing of what I had found was the journey completed, the circle closed. (pp. 118–119)

This group remembered the day and shared it with classmates through looking at projected slides of themselves in the snow, which I had taken. Using slides is another way to maintain a "strong umbilical cord," as Vea Vecchi says, between their experience outdoors and their memories and images of it. They moved into the slides, with the snow images projecting on them and danced their memories.

Later in the week, we invited children to choose materials with us that would be evocative of the snowy walk. Together we chose whites, and blues and grays from the tempera paint cart. We chose a sturdy, semitransparent roll of vellum as a background paper. We selected small pieces of lacy white doilies, and other feathery white papers from the collage drawer, along with some small pieces of clear acetate and lucite. Finally, we assembled the collection of drawing sticks they had brought in with them. All these materials could be used to represent the cold, blue day, the soft snow, the clear ice, and the fun of drawing in the snow with sticks. Five or six different children, including some who did not go on our particular walk, worked on the mural over a period of several days. They painted side by side on the floor, mostly enjoying the liquid winter colors, the feel of the "snow and ice" collage materials, and the effect of drawing in the paint with sticks as they had drawn in the snow. In the end, what the children made was an impression of their experience in our winter surroundings that we had explored together (see Figure 4.8).

Inventing New Paint Colors

One snowy morning four children who had chosen to paint in the *atelier* began by looking at photographs of snowflakes and frosted leaves with me and a student teacher. What colors did we see? What patterns and shapes? Together we chose tempera colors we thought would best represent these frosted colors and the muted snow world in the photographs and outside our classroom. We chose a variety of whites, grays, blues, lavenders, and muted greens.

The following exchange of ideas emerged as two 4-year-old boys painted side by side at the easel. We were fascinated as we listened to their predictions of what would happen to the colors as they blended, to their inventions of new

FIGURE 4.8. The Snowy Day Mural

names for colors, and to the drama and excitement of their conversation. Shannon and J.P. each began by working on their own painting. They became so involved in each other's work that they joined each other at the same easel and began to paint together (see Figure 4.9). Neither of these two boys had spent much time painting before. This day, they stayed for an hour and a half. These are excerpts from their conversation on January 25, 1995.

Shannon: The rain is coming down and making snowflakes. A snow storm is coming (*making quick marks in a downward motion with light-blue paint*).

J.P.: There are different snowflakes. This one has lines and dots. This one is like a snowflake but it is an "X." One is getting blown away. The long one is an icicle (*painting crosses with four to six lines, decorative dots, and a long vertical line as he changed from blue to white to gray paint*). The gray color is a cloudy snowstorm.

(After they have joined each other and begun to mix colors)

J.P.: The colors we mixed look like strawberry ice cream.

Shannon: Now it looks like chocolate ice cream.

J.P.: Snowflakes are all white but some need color like red. Let's see what happens when we put white on red snowflakes.

Shannon: It looks like cherry-lemon color. J.P., look what happened! It turned pink.

J.P.: The blue is cutting its way through the white. These snowflakes are very, very different.

Shannon: Look what happens when you put one color on top of another color.

J.P.: The purple looks like chocolate mixed up with plum.

Shannon: Look what happens when you mix purple. It is a giant waterfall. What do you think will happen when we add white to purple?

J.P.: This could be a sculpture. The blue is cutting its way through all the colors.

Shannon: I like working with paint. I'll paint pink and you can paint over the pink to get a new color.

J.P.: Blue on top of green makes brown.

Shannon: This area looks like Florida and that looks like South America with all the different shapes. The paint smells like chocolate, blueberry, and banana.

J.P.: This is a grape flavor.

Shannon: Now a tornado has come through the whole picture.

J.P.: It is a color picture. We made all new colors!

During the morning together, these two boys invented and named many new colors—strawberry, cherry-lemon, plum, cutting blue, blueberry, banana, and grape. The names are powerfully evocative of one of their favorite foods—ice cream. In fact, they end up speaking of the taste and smell of the paint. The immediacy of the colors and the strength of their associations leads them to cross sensory modes.

Figure 4.9. J.P. and Shannon at the Easel

They made other discoveries—white on red makes pink, or "cherry-lemon," blue on top of green makes brown, and strong blue dominates the other colors. They quickly moved from the frost and snow beginning into the drama of color mixing, which completely engaged them. It is as if the colors had come alive. In a morning, the two of them discovered the pleasure and the expressive power of paint as well as the joy of inventing together. They will be back.

Making Places and Telling Stories with Clay

One of our goals for the first year was to introduce clay to the preschool children and to present it over time in new ways so that children would learn increasingly rich and complex ways to use and interact with it. Clay was the primary "new" material that we planned to work with during the year.

When we introduced clay at the College School, it was new not only to the children, but also to the teachers, who had been accustomed to using plastic media such as playdough and "goop." I should note here that there is a strong visual arts program at the College School, but that the preschool children had been only peripherally involved in it. Before I arrived, preschool children had visited the art room for approximately 20 minutes a week. During these visits, they had some exposure to clay, but because their contact with the medium was limited and sporadic, they did not have the chance to get to know it very well or to use it for their own purposes. (Now, the art teacher and I work closely together so there is continuity in the children's experience and collaboration between us, the children, and the other teachers.)

In the beginning, as we brought clay into the classroom for everyday use, we were interested to see what the children would do with the clay on their own with little direction or suggestion from a teacher. When it was first presented to a group of 4- and 5-year-olds, several children said, "This is gushy, like mud." On individual clay boards, from grapefruit-sized portions of clay, many children began by making pies, cakes, hot dogs, and weapons. They spent quite a bit of time pounding the clay. During the second week, we offered them slip, explaining that it was like clay "glue" and that it could be used to hold pieces of clay together. They began by working for around 15 to 20 minutes at a time.

Then one day, about 2 weeks after it was first introduced, one child announced, "Today, I'm not making a cake. I'm going to make a sculpture." She began to form and smooth hills of clay and attach small pieces to larger mounds with the slip.

After discussing it together as teachers, we decided to vary the way we presented the clay to the children from time to time, to entice them to consider further possibilities with coils and slabs, building with the clay by adding to a base, and sculpting by digging in or taking away from a mound of clay. At the same time, we hoped to encourage small groups of children to work together in collaboration.

One day we put out several long coils of clay on a rectangular table along with a supply of fresh clay. The coils connected in several places and one coil looped up to make a bridge over another. At the morning meeting we asked if a group of four would like to work together to make something. It was a popular choice and four boys eagerly began to work. They made more coils—skinny ones and fat ones. They formed balls of clay of different sizes and flattened some into circles. They made connections, gave each other tasks, and together built roads, bridges, and islands, creating a complex and beautiful network. They collaborated for over an hour. They explained what they had made to all of us before lunch. Other children were excited to try working in this way some other day.

Another way we presented the clay to the children was in the form of slabs. We encouraged them to use the slabs as a base, almost like a piece of paper, to build up from. They shaped little balls of various sizes, flat pieces, and coils, and used slip to build small clay stories. Some children wanted to carve into the slab, so we began to experiment with digging into, taking away from, and imprinting in the clay with tools and natural materials like shells, acorns, and sticks. Some children wanted to include these materials in their clay pieces. At this point, we were able to begin to fire some of the children's favorite pieces in the school kiln. The white, bisque-fired pieces reminded me of coral or of tiny ocean floor worlds.

Their work was becoming more complex and more refined. More than half of the 24 children in the room now worked at the clay table with some regularity. They typically concentrated for over an hour, whether they worked collaboratively or independently. Sometimes they invented fanciful stories to go with their clay pieces, sometimes they did not. Their knowledge of the material and their skill in using it was growing. At the same time, they were deeply engaged in play: play in the sense of weaving stories and dramas out of real-life and imaginary possibilities, or experimenting with placing shapes and forms in ever-changing relationships. Whether their inclination was toward creating drama or making pattern and design in space, the clay offered them a rich, very open-ended material with which to shape their worlds.

Spook Mountain

One morning, when three boys chose to work with clay, they asked if they could have a big mound of clay, bigger than they had ever worked with. Together, we decided on the amount—about 40 pounds! The boys began to create what became Spook Mountain—a complex of tunnels and bridges, passageways and doors, entrances and exits, wrong turns and dead ends. They constructed the clay piece and the story together. They did not always agree about how the story would go or how Spook Mountain would take shape. They needed to come to compromise and resolution in order to continue. We covered Spook Mountain with wet cloths and a plastic bag to keep it moist overnight because the project extended itself over days. The children worked on Spook Mountain for approximately an hour a day, 5 days in a row.

They used their growing knowledge of the medium to create the complexity they envisioned—again, a network of relationships, a scary place that was full of dreadful possibilities, yet over which they had control. They were the masters of the universe, which to them at the time was embodied in the place they were creating—Spook Mountain.

The Mouse Hotel

Soon after, two girls asked for a large amount of clay to work with as well. For them, this ended up being around 15 pounds. They had been impressed with the boys' creation and thought they would try their hand at creating a special place as well. What materialized for them was a rounded structure with tunnels and special "rooms" inside, with configurations of thin coils and balls and flat, rounded shapes on the outside. Soon after they started, they began to refer to their clay piece as "The Mouse Hotel" (see Figure 4.10). The two girls worked on it for several weeks, adding new rooms and new dimensions to the elaborate story they were weaving.

We were very interested in their story and the carefully created clay spaces and forms they were making. We tape recorded some of their conversations as they worked, and we interviewed them when they were close to finishing the mouse dwelling. I am indebted to Nancy Nistler, a student teacher at the time, for recording and transcribing the tapes. The following is an excerpt from some of these conversations:

Nancy: Would you tell me about the rooms in the Mouse Hotel?
Meredith: Well, there is a cook room and a sleeping room and a dining room and there's the restaurant.
Elysia: There are lots of different doors. Here is the big door for moms and

FIGURE 4.10. Building the Mouse Hotel

dads and this is the hole for the babies. This door is for when you're coming in from playing (*pointing to the various different holes*).

Meredith: The babies sleep on the first floor. There are lots of cribs in there.
People go down to eat dinner there too and then they go to play outside.
This is the table right here.

Nancy: And what is behind this door?

Elysia: That is the bathtubs. The mice are this small (*gesturing with her index
finger and thumb*). They can go through that little door.

Nancy: What is this smaller ball here?

Meredith: That's the round door.

Nancy: Where does the round door lead?

Elysia: It leads to the creepy room where all the big kids go for their parties.

Meredith: And they don't let the babies go because they'll start crying.

Nancy: What are these little bowls on top of the hotel?

Meredith: This is a "bell pot." This is the clangor to call the mice with. When
they want to use it for cooking, they turn it over and use it as a pot.

Nancy: How did you two collaborate so well to build this together?

Elysia: Because we had a story of it.

Nancy: You had a story?

Meredith: I want to tell you about the eggs. These are the eggs. These are the
containers for the eggs. The most special egg in the Mouse Hotel is inside
here but you can't see it (*pointing to the most intricate part of the
hotel*).

Nancy: What makes it so special?

Meredith: There are lots of little eggs inside this egg.

Elysia: And they are little golden eggs.

Meredith: That makes it special.

Elysia: There is a very, very, very tiny golden egg. And when it cracks, a little,
little baby bird comes out.

Meredith: The bird is half gold. Its beak is gold.

Elysia: And half is silver. And it turns into a colored bird with black and white
and all the colors of the earth, the whole earth.

Meredith: But its beak is gold and the legs and feet are clear silver.

Elysia: And its wings get big, and it flies very gentle so it won't break the
clouds. It flies to Golden Land.

Meredith: It's probably as big as an eagle. Right, Elysia? Eagles are bigger than
crows.

Elysia: Now, the egg is in a basket with a cover over it and a cover over the
basket.

Meredith: He's the most important bird in the world.

This is an extraordinary tale of everyday family life, including care of
babies, dealing with big kids, eating dinner, playing outside, and taking baths—
all on the diminutive scale of mouse size. Then, the story turns to fairy tale,
telling of a mythical, magical bird yet to be hatched, which has found its place
in among the mice.

How did a lump of clay engage these two girls for 2 weeks and why did it
hold such meaning for them? In *Rose Garden and Labyrinth*, Seonaid Robertson
(1963) speaks of a story told by a young girl about a magical rose garden made

of a circle of lumps of clay, which she had lovingly formed. No one else would ever see the beauty or give the same significance to the clay pieces. The significance was in the power of the medium to hold a story of great significance to her. The story was told because she had the opportunity to work with the clay.

I believe it is the same for Elysia and Meredith. They love the clay. They are held by its plasticity and by their growing ability to give it the form they want. They are held by each other and the story they are telling together. They are held by their friendship, which is growing stronger as they develop their story, manage their mouse world, and shoulder the responsibility of protecting a mythical, kind, and gentle bird that is the most important bird in the world. They have entered into each other's imagination and perhaps tapped into the archetypal symbol that represents fragility and power at the same time (Jung, 1964). We can see the bird in our imaginations—all the colors of the earth, flying with giant wings and a golden beak so as not to break the clouds.

The clay, the time, the support, the climate of the classroom, and the appreciation and wonder of their teachers gave Elysia and Meredith the chance to do all these things. Indeed, all of the stories told here about children and their experiences with graphic materials, paint, and clay demonstrate the great potential that children have to use materials both to make sense of their varied experiences and to carry them toward new understanding and insight about the world and about themselves.

CHAPTER 5

Transforming Space, Time, and Relations

Hairy Vetch 6/28
BreadLoaf Barn

The educators of Reggio Emilia believe that the community deserves a school in which each member feels welcomed, needed, and engaged by exciting possibilities for learning and expressing ideas in "a hundred different languages." They believe community members, and especially parents, have the right to be informed about and involved in the wealth of activity that unfolds in the school daily. The Italian educators feel it is their responsibility to create a space and to provide the time for children, teachers, and parents to interact and collaborate with one another and to learn together about the wonder of the workings of the world. In this chapter, I will tell stories of change at the College School that focus on the classroom environment and the organization of our work with children, with colleagues, and with parents. We have learned that real change in any one of these areas both requires and inevitably effects change in the others. To make major changes in the classroom environment and to work productively alongside children and with each other within the new structures, we needed a new organization as a staff and, at the same time, we needed the understanding and participation of the parents.

TRANSFORMING THE SPACE OF THE PRESCHOOL

During the past 4 years, the teachers, parents, children, and the maintenance and administrative staffs of the College School have built the new and ever-evolving preschool space with hands, minds, and voices through many challenging yet rewarding periods. The story of the place and the way we have learned to live in it is not finished and will never be finished. At this point, however, we have learned enough and have gained adequate perspective to share our story.

How have we come to understand the meaning of the fundamental principle of the Reggio Approach: "the environment is the third teacher"? What have we learned through our reading, our visits to Reggio Emilia, and our intensive work at the College School with our friend and consultant from Reggio Emilia, Amelia Gambetti? What can we share about our daily practice of rethinking the space, questioning each other about children and how we think they learn, about parents and how they might best become our partners? What knowledge is bound up in the history of the layers of change in each tiny corner of the space at the College School?

We now know that the environment is a valuable teacher if it is amiable, comfortable, pleasing, organized, clean, inviting, and engaging. This is true of all space, whether big or small, open or furnished, public or private. This is true of floor space, ceiling space, and wall space.

The environment as educator is full of variety, with large spaces and small spaces, spaces for building, for dancing, for pretending, for talking, for wondering, and for reflecting. There are places for organizing, finding, and working with materials of all kinds. There are spaces for big groups and for small groups to think and imagine and make things together in a setting where both teacher and child can concentrate without distraction or interruption. Each space and each small corner of every space has an identity, a purpose, and it is cared for and respected by children and adults. We have learned, especially through our work with Amelia, that no space is marginal, no corner is unimportant, and each space needs to be alive, flexible and open to change.

Further, an environment that educates, holds the presence of all those who live, work, and play within it, even when they are not there. It speaks of their presence through their ideas expressed in drawing, clay, sculpture, words, and numbers. It speaks of their presence through their photographs and their names. The environment as educator has something to say—it communicates through the clear voices of children, teachers, and parents the depth of the learning and the thinking that take place in it. The voices are rich and varied and speak in many languages—the languages of numbers, words, sculpture, and graphics, to name a few.

We have learned from Carlina Rinaldi (1992) and through our own experience that the environment is the best educator when it promotes complex, varied, sustained, and changing relationships between people, the world of experience, ideas, and the many ways of expressing ideas. The best environment encourages this layered web of relationships to develop and grow.

To quote Carlina, "The best environment for children is one where the quality and quantity of relationships is as high as possible." When Carlina says "relationships," I interpret this to mean relationships between people—children, teachers, and parents; between people and materials and languages—words, numbers, pens, paper, clay, paint, wood; between people and ideas; and between people and experience with the world in which they live. In the philosophy of the Reggio Approach, the world should not be simplified but rather celebrated by adults and children in all its complex beauty.

We did not understand all this when we began at the College School. Even if we had, we would have started as we did with small attempts. We moved furniture and arranged displays of smooth stones and shells. We created places for parents and children to feel at home together. We created an *atelier* area as best we could. A parent architect designed and built a light table. We assembled new, high-quality drawing materials and papers on accessible shelves. We introduced clay, a clay table, and clay tools. We used an old wooden desk as our first message center and cardboard shoe holders as our first mailboxes. During the first year, as we tried to work in new ways together, we talked and argued over ideas about space, time, and collaboration. To be honest, we were overwhelmed and exhausted much of the time.

Amelia Gambetti visited for the first time in the spring of 1993. She came as a presenter to the consortium of schools supported by the Danforth grant and not as a consultant, although she did visit our school. I remember one comment of Amelia's about the housekeeping corner. She said, "Try to do something special with that area—something that can be identified with your personality in this school and that is unique to you. Everywhere I go in this country they all look the same. Do you all order from the same catalogue?"

Response and Advice from Reggio Emilia

The first major change in the space happened during the summer of 1993, after I had worked for a year at the College School. That spring, Brenda Fyfe and I had returned to Reggio Emilia with a second delegation from St. Louis. While we were there, we had the opportunity to give a presentation of our "work in progress" in St. Louis to some of the educators in Reggio Emilia. Approximately 25 teachers and administrators came, including the *equipe*, the group of all the *pedagogisti* (Carlina Rinaldi, Tiziana Fillipini, Sergio Spaggiari, and Loris Malaguzzi), and also three *atelieristi*—Giovanni Piazza, from La Villetta School; Vea Vecchi, from the Diana School; and Mara Davoli, from Neruda School.

After we gave an overview of our project in St. Louis and a comprehensive description of the changes and the process of change as experienced at the College School, the Reggio educators responded. Malaguzzi, in particular, had many things to say and we listened with interest.

Malaguzzi commented that many of our classrooms looked like attics. What did he mean? Mara suggested later that perhaps he saw large spaces with lots of furniture (and stuff), not much light, and not enough potential for different uses. Perhaps he saw no spaces for children to be private, no space (like the mini-*atelier*) for a small group of children to concentrate away from the noise of the group, and no space for a teacher to concentrate with a small group to research ideas or work with clay, paint, or other materials. He saw uniform heights of furniture, and not much attention to order or to function of the furniture, the equipment, or the materials. He did not see an effort to make the areas attractive in order to capture the attention of the children. An attic is protected from the outside world. It does not permit or invite interaction with the out-of-doors as the schools in Reggio Emilia do with their many interior and exterior windows, interior gardens, and classroom doors leading outside.

Carlina had similar comments. She said that it is necessary to look at the rights of children for the best space, for their best growth, not because the teachers in Reggio require it for their approach, but because we need to be clear with ourselves about what is best for children and best for teachers. Carlina said she didn't believe that it is acceptable to continue to adapt and adapt, but that at some point it is necessary to break with the old and create the new. She did not mean that we all have to build new schools, but that we need to change old spaces into the best possible spaces by making radical changes. This requires more than simply moving furniture around. To proceed with change, she suggested the following steps: one, to convince people why change is necessary; two, to decide what can be done; three, to find resources and financing.

Everyone at the presentation agreed that it would be more effective to focus on one school. This school could then be the focal point for all schools; it would serve as a place to work together, to have a common focus, to meet more often, to create links among teachers, to create consistency in goals, and to create a viable model.

When I spoke with Vea Vecchi later that week, she quoted Malaguzzi, "For plants to thrive and flourish, they need the best conditions. Your children do also."

The honest responses of the educators in Reggio Emilia, especially those of Loris Malaguzzi and Carlina Rinaldi, convinced us that it was time to make major changes in our space. Brenda and I returned to St. Louis with great determination and enthusiasm. We knew we would need to find a way to convince others, most critically Jan Phillips, the director of the College School, of the vision and the need for change.

The Architectural Program

Our enthusiasm must have been contagious. Jan seemed excited and willing to investigate ways to improve our space. She suggested that we all meet with Frank and Gay Lorberbaum, who were College School parents and architects. The first thing that Gay and Frank asked us to do was to write a "program." This is an architectural term meaning a description of what the client wants and needs in a space. Gay gave me permission to use any kind of language I wanted, to talk about the kind of feel we were after, even to talk about intangible things we wanted from the space. She emphasized that it need not be written in design, architectural, or mathematical language. What follows are excerpts from the program that I wrote in the spring of 1993.

> Gay has insisted, quite rightly, that those of us involved in this work write a program. By that, she means a "psychological, functional, lyrical description" of what we want and feel we need in a space if we are to continue to grow and begin to flourish in our understanding and practice of this approach. She suggested that we not limit ourselves to the confines of the present space, rather, that we let our imaginations soar.
>
> We are ready to go forward. I think we all have the strong feeling that we need conditions to change. We need and want the space to reflect our growth and to encourage the development of the full capabilities of the adults and children who live in it. Further, and perhaps more important, to allow us to move beyond where we've come, our environment must change. Somehow, the present space is disrespectful of our collective intelligence and creativity. It holds us down. It does not support our work.
>
> 1. We need light. Small amounts of light coming from smoky, old windows stuffed with ugly air-conditioners makes our space seem more like a prison than a school. When I go to Dorris's room in the morning, I want to curl up like a cat on the floor, relishing the one patch of light that graces our two rooms. I love the tall, elegant windows in the fourth-grade classroom upstairs. Besides welcoming natural light, they allow us to participate in the life of the grand old oak outside through all its transformations.
>
> 2. In addition to natural light, we need harmonious, pleasant artificial light.
>
> 3. The steel-gray walls feel more suited to a factory than a school. We would love the walls painted a bright, warm white instead of gray.
>
> 4. We wish for a beautiful floor; one that is lovely to walk on, playful, and inviting to sit on. We spend quite a bit of time on the floor as preschool teachers and children. The floor needs to be a pleasant color and a solid base from which to build. Perhaps we need more carpet.
>
> 5. We need some height to the ceiling. It hangs over us like low clouds, not allowing for lofty thoughts or dreaming upward gazes. It simply contains us. The variation of ceiling height and the transparency

of so many interior and exterior windows at the Diana and La Villetta Schools are an inspiration to the spirit and to the intelligence.

6. We need transparency. The heavy walls that separate the two preschool rooms inhibit the collaboration that we are trying to achieve. This is also true of the walls that separate us from the rest of the school.

7. We need an inviting entrance area, for parents, children, and the rest of the school. At present, one steps into the preschool through darkly stained, heavy wooden doors and enters a windowless, joyless room. We would like to see the entrance welcome people as soon as they arrive and invite collaboration between teachers, children, and parents. This could be a space for children to mingle with peers and adults and the other children in school.

8. We need to break up our cavernous spaces into inviting, irresistible areas "like market stalls," as Malaguzzi often calls them. Thoughtfully planned areas of the classroom would include a platform for small-block building with storage bins underneath, an open area for moving to music and experimenting with sounds and instruments, a private dress-up/housekeeping corner set apart with attractive partitions, a comfortable, orderly book corner, and attractive tables throughout the room for working on projects.

9. We need to clear out the unnecessary junk from closets and the classroom. We need to create a space and place for everything that is important to the function of the classroom. We need a clear sense of order, beauty, and purpose and a way to maintain it.

10. We need an *atelier* or studio/workshop—a space set apart by transparent walls where teachers could work with small groups of children and not be distracted. The *atelier* would be big enough to include a square or rectangular adult-sized table for 10 adults and/or children to meet comfortably, a large, mural-sized floor space for working, and deep shelving made to hold a variety of sizes of paper and equipment, as well as metal shelving for smaller, more accessible materials, and a utility sink.

Structural Change

With this program and a collection of images of the schools in Reggio Emilia in hand, Gay and Frank designed an *atelier* and new plans for the entryway, which addressed almost all of the needs we had specified (see Figure 5.1). The renovations took place in the summer of 1993. Three half-walls, from 3 feet off the floor to the ceiling, in the front entry came out and were replaced with glass windows made of 2-foot-square modular sections. Each module is rimmed with 3-inch sills on all four sides. The bottom sills are ideal for display of natural materials and clay sculpture.

The *atelier* was defined by a new floor-to-ceiling glass wall, also constructed in 2-foot-square modular sections. This new wall divides the large space of the classroom of the 4- and 5-year-olds into two spaces and creates the *atelier*. The heavy, dark, double doors leading to the room of the 3- and 4-year-olds were replaced with a similar glass wall on the other side of the new *atelier*

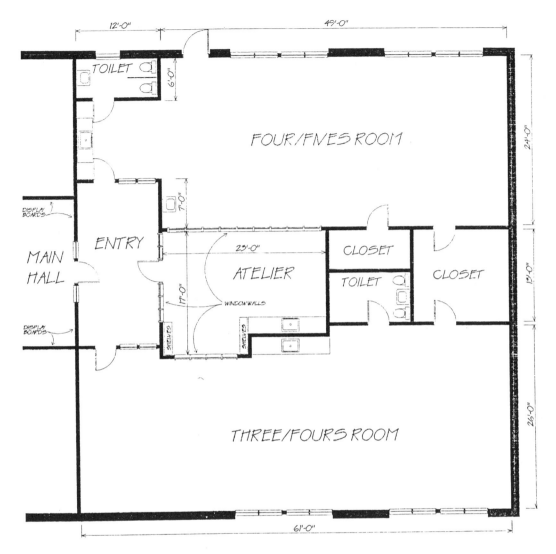

FIGURE 5.1. The Plan of the Preschool

space. Instead of acoustic tiles in the *atelier* ceiling, we now have mylar tiles and new lighting with parabolic reflectors. These relatively inexpensive mylar tiles, along with the reflectors, have created the illusion of height and variety in the ceiling and attract and reflect light in every direction throughout the entire space of the preschool (see Plate 3).

In place of the worn, beige floor there is now a soft, aqua bluegreen linoleum tile that reflects its watery color in the new ceiling. Built-in shelves line both sides of the alcove created from the area that was formerly the passageway between classrooms.

These structural changes cost the College School $10,000, which was raised in large part from the school's capital improvement budget and in part from parent donations. The decision to make these dramatic changes demonstrated a new level of commitment to our work on the part of the administration and the board of directors and set the stage for deeper levels of change.

The construction of the *atelier* was the beginning of the miraculous metamorphosis that has since taken place. Even though there are the same number of windows to the outside as before, the interior windows, the mirrored ceiling, and the new fluorescent lighting create the illusion that there is an abundance of natural light. The dark, dreary space of the preschool has been completely transformed into a light-filled, sparkling, well-organized, and engaging environment. Likewise, the way in which we, the adults and children, live our lives in this space has been transformed as well. We all, children and teachers and parents, live in the space as home. We are all comfortable. We are respectful of each other and all the materials in the space. We are all engaged in exciting, ongoing inquiry. And we are all, adults and children together, continually inspired to seek and discover, construct and interpret that which matters in our lives. Our experience confirms Jim Greenman's (1988) strong statement in the opening pages of his book, *Caring Spaces, Learning Places: Children's Environments That Work.*

> An environment is a living, changing system. More than the physical space, it indicates the way time is structured and the roles we are expected to play. It conditions how we feel, think, and behave; and it dramatically affects the quality of our lives. (p. 5)

WORKING WITH AMELIA

I was privileged to spend the second half of my internship in Reggio Emilia with Amelia Gambetti, a teacher of 25 years in the Reggio Emilia preschools, and her class of 5- and 6-year-olds. This period was intensely busy for her because from February through June 1992, Amelia was a leader, along with Giovanni Piazza, Carlina Rinaldi, and Loris Malaguzzi, in the now well-known project, "The Amusement Park for Birds" (1994), which was documented in video format by George Forman and Lella Gandini. During this time, Amelia and I came to know each other well and often dreamed of working together in the United States.

After retiring from her job in the schools in Reggio Emilia, Amelia made it known that she would like the chance to work with teachers in schools in the United States. George Forman was able to offer her a job as lead consulting teacher at the University of Massachusetts Lab School in Amherst in 1992–93. During the next 2 years she served as lead consultant at the Model Early Learning Center in Washington, DC. (The Model Early Learning Center has since become a reference point for us through visits, exchanges, and consultations with the teachers there.) During these 3 years she traveled to many states and over 100 schools, giving workshops and seminars on the Reggio Approach.

By the time she came to us, she was familiar with American ways of thinking about preschools and preschool children. In some ways, she knew what to expect and how to tackle what, in the beginning, must have seemed to her like almost insurmountable barriers. At the College School, we did not have a lot of time to work together. We did, however, have the advantage of my intense period of learning in her school in Italy, our common experience in working cross-culturally, and our friendship.

Amelia is full of energy and intense commitment to the values and principles that have grown and developed in Reggio Emilia as she grew and developed as a teacher researcher. She is extraordinarily gifted in her ability to point out the presence or absence of those values and principles in every aspect of life in a school.

Amelia is small, with blond hair and sparkling brown eyes. She has a commanding presence, and she is a demanding person. She often says, "But I am demanding first with Amelia." She does not mince words, and she does not waste time. In part, she learned this style of working under the mentorship of Loris Malaguzzi and Carlina Rinaldi. Working with Amelia is intense, and exhausting, but it is the most satisfying work most of us have ever done. I have always been gratful that she has been willing to bring all of herself and all she knows to the task of working with American teachers. Those of us who have worked closely with her now have a responsibility to share what and how we have learned with others in the most direct way possible.

We began our serious work with Amelia in the spring of 1994, when she consulted with us for one week. She spent the first day touring every corner of our space, taking notes and observing what was happening around her. On the second day of her visit, she began to talk to me about what she did and did not see. She wanted to work closely with me first because of our mutual experience and understanding and because my time was more flexible than that of the rest of the teachers. She suggested we start together in one space, roll up our sleeves, and begin. She knew that I needed to understand what she wanted to tell me through action and experience. What follows is the story of our work in the entryway of the preschool, which we now call the living room.

"The Environment Is the Third Teacher."

As we walked into the entryway Amelia commented that there were many animals—fish, guinea pigs, and birds—and natural materials in the preschool and in the College School in general. She suggested that nature and an emphasis on the environment were strong and unique characteristics of the school. She said we should emphasize this even more—organize materials and spaces to communicate this identity as clearly as possible. She pointed to a wooden table just inside the door, which had a plant and a basket of pine cones on it. "What could you do there?" "Add more, make it more engaging and interesting," I suggested. "Exactly," nodded Amelia.

On one wall of the entryway there is a floor-to-ceiling mural of a tree in several shades of browns and greens, which had been designed and painted by an adult. "Let's give this tree more of a reason for being," said Amelia.

> What about moving that flight cage of finches that is in the hall in here in front of it. That would solve several problems . . . it would give the tree a purpose—a backdrop for the birds; it would make the birds feel closer to the out-of-doors—near the colors and image of a tree; and it

would leave you a space on the display board just outside the preschool entrance to develop a functioning parent information board, which you are clearly missing.

The embarrassing truth is that the flight cage had been moved from another location in the school and had been temporarily placed in front of our first attempt at a parent communication board. It had been there for over a month, covering the only visible presence of parents in our preschool. On her first day, looking for the parent board, Amelia finally had found it behind the birds! (A teacher who saw her taking notes in front of the cage was impressed that she was such an avid bird watcher.)

That day, we moved the flight cage to the new location, where it has remained. "Now," Amelia told me, "you could have a project for which there is no end. Imagine the possibilities for investigating and getting to know these birds."

At the time, we were involved in a study of two toads that had come to live in our classroom at the beginning of the year. Amelia suggested moving the terrarium with the toads onto the table with the natural materials. "Then the toads also will have a more friendly environment—they will be surrounded by natural materials." When I questioned moving the panels about the toad story out into the entryway because I thought I could do it on my own after she had left, she stopped to look at me and said slowly, "I am trying to help you understand each step we are making and why. We need to do it now so we can look at the whole room together and then you can talk to the other teachers about what we have done and why we have done it." I understood.

We relocated the panels as close to the toads as possible. "In this way, people understand that you and the children are friends with these toads and that you are learning about them. But you need a title for your panels and a paragraph introducing the story and explaining why you, as teachers, think it is important. You could put it right here," she said, pointing out a logical spot.

As a final touch, Amelia found a philodendron plant in a white basket, which she placed on top of a shelf in the corner and trained up the wall in between the panels. The small plant connects the natural world with the represented world of words, photographs, and the paintings and drawings the children had made during the investigations about their toad friends.

An antique piano sat in the opposite corner of the entryway. We now turned our attention to it. A portable board on the top of the piano rested against the wall. We were using it to display drawings children had done during an investigation of their features—their particular noses, eyes, mouths, and ears.

Amelia's first question was, "What is that?" I explained as best I could, but Amelia probed farther.

Do you think this is the best way to present the children's work and your work? What is the context? I don't understand. Did the children do any full portraits of themselves during this investigation? What did they say about themselves? Where are their voices? Don't you think that you need a title? Where is your reflection on this work as teachers? Were the parents involved at all? Did the children do any research about faces at home with their parents? What does this board communicate?

I had to say that it communicated that children were doing interesting drawings, but that the drawings were out of context. The board looked messy. It was hard to make sense of it.

Later we put together a strategy with my colleague Jennifer who had initiated this work with the children. We decided that Jennifer should plan to finish the work with small groups of children, in a place where they could focus with plenty of time. Then together she and I would add the missing pieces, write an introduction, and organize a group of panels on self-portraits. Amelia encouraged us to continue to enrich and deepen the exploration of self through other languages such as movement, shadow play, and clay. These were the first pieces of documentation we planned, designed, and carried out as a team. It was the beginning of our understanding of the value, for both children and adults, of important, well-thought-out experiences with children and the clear, well-articulated communication of those experiences.

We continued at the piano. Amelia found several baskets of dried flowers and arranged them on top of the piano. She suggested we hang a Matisse poster that we found behind the piano, above it. She asked, "Now, what does it look like to you?" I said it looked like home. "Yes, and you might want to continue to make it look and feel more like home by adding a table with a small lamp. Also, think about other instruments and how they might be a part of this corner."

We sat down on the small couch against the wall facing the bird cage and admired each area of the space. There was a sense that the room had been "characterized," as Amelia says. It was beginning to have a personality and an identity. There was a home for the birds, a home for the toads, a clear, readable story about the toads, a context for the tree mural, and an inviting music corner.

From here, Amelia continued to examine the space. She looked up and noticed a small bulletin board crammed with small forgotten notes and lists. "What's that for?" she inquired. "It's awful." We cleared the board and filed or threw out the papers. Amelia looked in the *atelier* and choose a small collage made of various green tissue papers made at the light table earlier in the week to put on the board. We both appreciated the simple, single piece on a board just the right size for it. I thought, "No space is unimportant, no space is marginal."

Continuing to look around, Amelia asked me what the cupboard was for next to the couch. "Why is it empty? This is a couch where you would like parents and children from both classes to sit and enjoy looking at books together. Wouldn't it be a good place for albums or books made by each class?"

She continued to question me.

What about each classroom? How do you know what age child is in the rooms? How do you know what teachers and which children are in each room? Do you think this is important? Why? Can all the children find themselves in photographs? Why don't you add a list of the names of children and teachers, in each class, a photograph of the class and teachers, and a title like, "3/4 Class," cut neatly out of acetate, for the window at the entry of each room?

To identify the *atelier* we cut letters out of blue acetate so that the words themselves would be transparent like the glass and therefore reflect the light. We composed a group of white, wintery transparent collages to put under the title on the glass door.

While we worked, some of the children had moved through the entry-way, some dropping dress-ups and toys. Amelia commented, "You need to help them understand that this is their entry. It needs to stay picked up and not left a mess. Even very young children have the capability to understand that they are free to play and to use the equipment and materials as long as they keep the area neat at the same time." This statement supports the image of a child who is strong, capable, and full of potential.

Finally, at the end of the morning, Amelia asked me what I thought of what we had done. I thanked her and said I thought I was better equipped to continue now that I had seen through her eyes and made so many kinds of changes with her. She said, "Look around. This is one example that illustrates why we call the environment 'the third teacher.' Now this room is alive, it has its own identity, and it speaks for itself."

Time, Organization, and Relations

The work in the entry describes the way in which we have begun to examine and re-examine each part of the preschool with Amelia and on our own. We finally have developed the habit of asking ourselves the same hard questions Amelia asks us. She has taught us to identify our motivation for every choice we make. She has helped us to train our minds and eyes to see in more exacting and careful ways than we did when we began this work. We have continued to change and work with every part of the space, questioning ourselves, observing children, and working with children and parents, to organize, enrich, and further characterize all the spaces in the preschool—the small- and the large-block areas, the communication and message centers, the *atelier*, the cubbies, the book corners and library, the meeting areas and risers, the kitchen area, the bathrooms, the parent communication boards, and the introduction to our school.

We have made changes in the space so that we can work in the most productive ways with children, with each other, and with parents. However, learning how to work well within the new spaces has presented other challenges for everyone involved. Although we have made continual progress, we are still struggling with issues of time, organization, collaboration, and the development of new skills as teachers. Over the 4 years, with Amelia's help, we have examined all of these issues from different perspectives many different times.

Since her first visit as a consultant, Amelia has visited St. Louis on four other occasions for a week at a time, with the exception of October 1995, when she worked for the entire month in all three schools in our network. Every time we have worked with her, we have deepened our understanding and our practice—our practice of continually creating and maintaining the environment as the third teacher; our practice of organizing the greatest number of the highest-quality experiences with children, with each other, and with parents; our practice of continuing to uncover the intricacies and the power of the hundred languages for children and also for ourselves; our practice of listening to, talking with, and observing children; and our practice of making the depth of children's thinking and our thinking visible and clear.

It seems as if we are on a spiraling journey on which we often circle back to the same issues; yet, since we have changed, we see the issues differently every time we re-examine them. Each time, we are ready to tackle something new because of our history of experience and our new perspectives. Amelia suggests that the consistency and continuity of our experience together have helped us to find our own identity as a group and a new way of thinking.

For example, we have begun to understand that for children's experiences to be as wonderful as possible, teachers need to reacquaint themselves with the wonder of the world and begin to see and understand it through children's eyes. If children are to speak their true thoughts and feelings about the world, teachers need to develop skills that will enable them to have valuable conversations with children. For children to develop and grow through all their natural languages, teachers themselves need to understand the potential of the languages and the qualities of the materials. In order to revisit and communicate the learning that takes place during these experiences with children, colleagues, and parents, teachers must develop skills in observing, recording, photographing, and reflecting. All of these skills and practices take time and patience to understand and to develop. At the three schools in St. Louis, we are supporting each other as we continue to struggle and to learn.

Building Collaboration as Colleagues

Having understood the first stages of these new approaches and practices, we are more aware than ever of our need for time together to discuss these new ways of working and to reflect and hypothesize about our experiences with children. Although we always knew we needed to be more organized to work successfully as collaborators and that we needed to find time to organize ourselves and our work, at first we did not seem to know how or where to start.

It is clear that in order to work collaboratively, teachers need enough time to think through and organize themselves for the time they will be with children. If children are to live experiences of the highest quality in school, we cannot improvise. Amelia often tells us that the more organized we are, the more room there will be for flexibility and for new possibilities in our work with children.

If this organizing is to be done collaboratively, it means meeting with colleagues to study something that one or two teachers have been following (for example, to share the evolution of an ongoing block structure or an experience following the birth of a new guinea pig). When the staff understands the scope and content of all the various experiences that are underway, they can help each other organize possible next steps in each experience and together they can orchestrate the days and weeks ahead: Who will follow which experience? How will these teachers make the experience as rich as possible? How will they observe, record, and photograph the experience? What support do they need from others?

We have discovered that we need to meet together as teachers every morning for half an hour before the children arrive, to look over the day, to make sure we know who is following which experience with how many children, and to share important information about unfolding experiences. Our morning meetings with children have evolved into similar times of sharing important, ongoing investigations, work, and wonderings in which the children often take the lead. Collaboratively, decisions are made about who will do what that day.

As colleagues, we also meet one afternoon a week for an hour while an assistant supervises the children's nap time. In addition, we meet one afternoon a week after school for 2 hours. We are learning how to use this time in a variety of ways. The longer meetings focus on looking ahead and organizing possibilities for small-group work, analyzing transcripts of conversations with children, as well as discussing difficulties, challenges, and problems that need group solutions. We keep minutes of these meetings, which go in a binder to be referred to as needed. The practice of keeping minutes gives us a tangible way to organize ourselves and provides a valuable record of our collaborative thinking.

As the weeks and years go by, we are beginning to sense what real collaboration feels like. When I was living in the midst of my days at the Diana and La Villetta Schools, I had no idea that the exquisite dance of collaboration I witnessed grew out of so many levels of skills, layers of common experience, and mutual trust among adults and children who embarked together daily on adventures of discovery. After 4 years, there are moments when I feel as if we may be beginning to learn to dance together in St. Louis.

FIGURE 5.2.   The Entrance to the Preschool in 1992

FIGURE 5.3. The Entrance to the Preschool in 1996

Transforming Relations with Parents

Although it will be impossible to fully describe it here, another area of organization and collaboration that needs to be mentioned is our work with parents. Amelia emphasized that in order to begin parent involvement in earnest, we needed to believe in the importance of working with parents and be prepared to accept the challenges involved as necessary to our growth as teachers. She also explained that we needed a structure—beginning with a parent–teacher committee, and the clear, visible presence of the parents through a thoughtfully organized parent communication board. We initiated the parent–teacher committee in the fall of 1994. Until then, we did not really understand the differences between our idea of parent involvement and the concept of parent involvement in Reggio Emilia.

Now, the parent–teacher committee, comprised of three or four parent volunteers from each classroom and three of the five teachers on our team, meets one afternoon each month after school. The task of this committee is to ensure that all parents feel a sense of belonging in the school, become involved in the community, and share the pleasure and the challenges of the extraordinary gift of parenthood and childhood with the other parents and with us.

Through our work during the past 2 years, we have come to understand what it means to have parents as partners. They are a respected and necessary voice in all that we do. Instead of merely organizing parties, driving on field trips, and being interested primarily in their own children, they know and understand what we do in school with all the children; they offer their skills in many ways, from sharing a hobby like cooking or carpentry to leading workshops for parents, to researching possibilities for project-related outings. Together, we plan and orchestrate celebrations with the children. Some have become yearly traditions like our pot-luck, musical holiday party where children and parents exchange handmade gifts.

All the parents are informed about daily life in school through various channels: our daily journal, written and illustrated by several children and a teacher, letters that go home from teachers and children, and minutes from the parent–teacher committee meetings and other small-group parent meetings, which are posted on the parent board. The parent communication board documents all of the many ways in which parents are involved in the school through photographs, quotes, calendars, and children's drawings. The board is still just outside the preschool where the bird cage used to be. The 4-year-long transformation of the hall leading to the preschool is apparent in Figures 5.2 and 5.3. As in every area of this approach, we continue to learn more about effective, meaningful parent involvement as we gain experience and taste the results and rewards of our efforts. The parents are helping us to do that.

So it is with Amelia's help that we continue our work, even when she is not here. And along with Amelia there is Malaguzzi, Carlina, Vea, Marina, Giovanni, and the whole community of educators, children, and parents in Reggio Emilia, Italy, who continue to inspire us and push us to examine everything we do and to continually question each other, always in the service of creating the highest-quality experience in school that is possible for children, for parents, and for ourselves on this side of the ocean.

CHAPTER 6

The Children and the Garden

7/10 Blackeyed Susans
lower meadow

The morning breeze is cool, rising from the earth, which is at long last saturated with water from yesterday's steady rain. The light air feels soft and fresh on my skin, almost a miracle after the dry, bristling heat of the last weeks. I listen to our friendly, local cardinal whistle his strong, vivid call from the old apple tree below and the mourning dove sing her slow, wistful song from the meadow nearby. The shadows of the apple leaves cast by the morning sun play on the wooden floor.

I have come outside to write on the front porch of our Vermont home as I begin this last chapter about place and voice in my life and in the lives of the children with whom I have lived and worked. I have come full circle. I have returned to the place from which we started 5 years ago. I have come home.

A few days ago, I took the time to admire the delicate, summertime blooms of the tiny periwinkle daisies that our friend Karen planted among the low rock walls that border our back terrace. Dainty, feathery flowers, deep, sky blue with a kiss of a yellow center, they cluster in sprays that grace the ridges and crevices of the gray stone. We are grateful to Karen for caring for our garden while we are away in St. Louis. The first few years of our absence, we spent the entire summers digging up and replanting what was left of our overgrown, cultivated beds. The wild meadow and thicket world that surrounds us is always eager to take over.

I remember this ridge before we built our house here, when it was thick with honeysuckle and sumac. These native shrubs had grown up around the old apple trees of the orchard that thrived here 50 years ago. In order to build, the land had to be cleared.

To create the foundation for our house, it was necessary to blast a cellar hole out of the ancient rock that shapes the ridge—a metamorphosed slate formed 4 hundred million years ago when a shallow sea covered this land. To me, the blast seemed a terrible thing at the time, shamelessly violating this wise, old rock. To blow it to smithereens because we wanted to live here seemed senseless. However, over the next months, the rock fragments of all sizes were moved and stacked by a back hoe, with my husband Ashley, the designer, directing, to form retaining and garden walls. Every piece of the rock that had been our cellar was put back together again in a new puzzle. The rock had taken a new form.

I think of Gary Snyder's (1979) words from his essay "The Place, the Region, the Commons."

> A place on earth is a mosaic within larger mosaics—the land is all small places, all precise, tiny realms replicating larger and smaller patterns. . . . The whole world is a great tablet holding multiple overlaid new and ancient traces of the swirl of forces. Each place is its own place, forever (eventually) wild. (p. 27)

We are privileged to have this gift of time here on the piece of wild land where we live. We have cultivated and enriched the earth, planted flowers and herbs, vegetables and trees. We have worked with the land. We have made a home. We have made a garden.

I used to love working in the garden with my own two children when they were young. They loved it too, for short periods of time. They planted tiny seeds with their little fingers, dug for worms in the dark earth, and watched the first small plants break through the soil with excitement and amazement. Later in the summer, they delighted in hiding in among the leaves of the pole beans and eating the crunchy, raw pods right off the vine. They loved pulling up the musty carrots and fiery radishes that had been hiding underground and picking small bouquets of zinnias and marigolds for the kitchen table.

The garden was a special world for them. Here, they could watch the miracle of a small seed's transformation from tender seedling, to mature plant, to food for our dinner, back to the compost pile. The garden became a place to explore the lives of other creatures that lived under the earth and on the plants— fat red worms, white spiders on yellow day lilies, the painted lady butterfly on the daisy. It was a place to hide under green leafy shelters in the heat of the summer. It was a place to snap peas from the vine and eat them, still warm from the sun and wet with dew.

Edith Cobb has written extensively about the visceral, sensory integration of self and the natural world we feel as children. She hypothesizes that our innate connection with nature in childhood and the poetic voice we find as children, are at the root of our creativity as adults. In her book, *The Ecology of Imagination in Childhood*, Cobb (1977) writes: "In childhood, the cognitive process is essentially poetic because it is lyrical, rhythmic, and formative in a generative sense; it is a sensory integration of self and environment" (p. 89).

Cobb suggests that the materials of the natural world, such as sand, twigs, and stones, can serve children in their "world-making" or "world-shaping" activities (p. 89). Children's need to build a relationship with the natural world can be nurtured both by using the earth's materials and through shaping small worlds of their own to inhabit in their imaginations.

I wanted to begin a project or "long story" with children at the College School that would afford them many chances for this kind of "world making" and relationship building with the natural world. I hoped to begin a project focused on the natural world, which would be comparable to the Tree Project I had followed and from which I learned so much in Reggio Emilia. At the same time, I knew the origins of this new project needed to be rooted in our work with children and in our place.

Because of my love of gardens, I considered the idea of investigating seeds and plants and possibly planting a garden as a likely topic. At a conference for writers and educators that I attended 2 years earlier, I remembered Richard Nelson (1994) saying:

> The best way to demonstrate to children that they are a living part of the ecological web is to have them eat something right off the land. If they see food only in supermarkets, they think that's where it comes from. I don't know of a better teacher than your stomach. Go out and pick or gather food you can eat together or just take your children outside and let them eat dandelions. (p. 10)

What follows is a narrative description of the beginnings of a project on plants that began in the preschool in February 1993 and continued into the kindergarten the following year. In recounting the beginnings of the project in the preschool, I am eliminating transcripts of conversations and detailed descriptions of teachers' and children's work. The story of the project in the preschool is meant to set the stage for the more detailed description and analysis of the project as it took shape in the kindergarten. I will discuss the project as it evolved in the kindergarten in depth, focusing particularly on the work of seven 5- and 6-year-old children. The work of these seven children actually continued beyond their kindergarten year as they planted and tended a summer garden with the partnership of their parents and their first-grade teacher.

In a sense, the kindergarten Garden Project represents the culmination of the first chapter of my efforts to study and adapt the Reggio Approach in an American school setting. It is also the fruition of my work of many years as a teacher who has studied children's language and visual symbols in order to better understand how to support children's development. Like the Tree Project at the Diana School in Reggio Emilia, the Garden Project nurtured children's growing relationship with the natural world of plants and helped them to develop a strong sense of place in an outdoor setting that they learned to love together.

TURNING THE PRESCHOOL CLASSROOM INTO A GREENHOUSE

As luck would have it, the family of a preschool child in the 4- and 5-year-old room owned a large commercial greenhouse and the father was particularly interested in helping out in the classroom. To begin with, he asked if he could bring in some soil with seeds for the children to plant. Later, he was eager to have us visit the greenhouse and to travel behind the scenes to the composting and growing areas. We arranged to take the children there in groups of six or eight. In this way, we could take the time to explore, without having to keep track of too many children or disturbing the employees or patrons of the greenhouse. We also would be better able to concentrate on what the children noticed and what their questions were.

Our first trip to the greenhouse was in February. It was cold and snowy outside. Inside, the air was moist and warm, filled with the smell of rich soil. The huge space was lined with row upon row of green and flowering plants— ivies in many varieties, ferns and orchids, hanging baskets of begonias and geraniums, and small fica, orange, and palm trees in a central, open area. The children wandered in among the plants, admiring them, their heads just above the tops of the plants. We visited the composting, soil-producing section of the greenhouse, where a friendly woman was concocting the greenhouse's own special soil—with turkey dung! We were led back into the "employees only" space, where children had a chance to plant a small begonia seedling and laugh under the sprays of water from the pipes of the watering system.

When we returned to school, the children told their classmates that the greenhouse was something like a jungle. Several children were so enamored with the green space we had visited that they said they wanted to turn our classroom into a greenhouse. Another child, who had been fascinated with the commercial aspect of the work of the greenhouse, added with excitement that we could then have a plant sale and invite the whole school! Many of her classmates were excited by the idea, and so were we as teachers. We all agreed to try.

Needless to say, these were exciting ideas and the beginnings of a possible long story. We spent the next weeks talking with children about the kinds of things they would like to grow and visiting a local nursery to select and purchase seeds and peat pots. Our greenhouse family generously donated a 25-pound bag of their best soil mixture. Since we had so much soil, a group of children wanted to fill an empty sand table with it and plant it as a small garden.

A committee of six 4- and 5-year-old children decided how the seeds should be planted, how many of each kind of seed, how many in each pot, and how we should organize the planting. When the plants began to sprout, we all realized, children and adults together, that the young plants seemed much healthier on the side of the preschool where we had morning sun. Together, we moved the table on wheels and all the peat pots and larger pots full of new peas and parsley, beans and lettuce into the 3- and 4-year-old children's classroom. The children were enthusiastic about watering regularly, with a little help from the adults in establishing a routine. They especially liked to mist the young plants with spray bottles. By mid-March, we were able to harvest and taste some cress, lettuce, and green beans.

During this time, children drew the growing plants in the same way they had drawn the leaves as subjects in the fall. They also began to draw and paint plant forms spontaneously. We arranged for small-group conversations together to discuss their ideas about the seeds and their growth. As the time for the plant sale drew near, we began to plan for it during our small- and large-group conversations.

At this point, we realized that we did not have many plants fit to sell. One child suggested that the greenhouse had lots of baby plants and maybe they would give us some. We decided with the children that clay pot vessels for the plants would make them even more special. After I showed them some simple techniques, children began to shape free-form slab and coil pots from red clay, which we bisque fired. The greenhouse donated small clay pots as well, which the children painted in decorative patterns with acrylic paints.

Many children hoped to invite their whole neighborhood to the plant sale, but in the end the children and teachers decided to limit the sale to the College School. A group of boys were eager to make a ''Preschool Plant Sale'' sign as a replacement for the school sign that hung above the entrance to our building. However, they compromised and made a very large banner to hang inside the school. Other children made posters announcing the sale and wrote letters to send home to parents. Two boys appointed themselves to announce the sale over the PA system and arranged to visit the director of the school to obtain permission to do so.

Another group, most interested in the financial aspects of the sale, determined how much the plants should cost and made appropriate tags. They asked several mothers to help them the day of the sale so that they could make the right change and handle the money as it came in.

The day finally arrived when everything was ready. Parents and students flocked to the sale, which was centrally located in the front entryway of the school. The preschool plant sellers, the publicity committee, and the welcomers were all there. The children's eyes grew wide when they saw paper dollars accumulating in the money box. With the support of their parents and teachers, their original idea had come true.

Because the last day of school was approaching, the money the children raised was not counted until the following fall. A group of five kindergarten students spent three hour-long sessions deliberating together and counting all the bills and the change that they had made at the plant sale. In the end, the total amounted to $67.38. The money was later used to buy seeds and to purchase materials for the kindergarten Garden Project.

As a memory of the story of both the leaves and plants in preschool, a group of children painted a mural during the last weeks of school that included many of their drawings and paintings of leaves and plant forms from throughout the year. I had learned this technique from Vea Vecchi at the Diana School and I was ready to try it with children.

The children and I began by enlarging the children's drawings of plants from throughout the year with the help of an overhead projector. We then moved the large drawings around a rectangular piece of mural paper until we decided on a starting composition that made sense to us. The next step was to place a sheet of transparent plastic over the mural paper design. The original drawings showed through and could be used as a guide for the acrylic paint that was painted right onto the plastic. Once the children began, they embellished and added to their original drawings. The mural still hangs in the *atelier* as a wonderful memory of that first year. The children who made it, now in second grade, still come to visit and to admire it (see Plate 4).

TAKING THE GARDEN PROJECT TO KINDERGARTEN

At the outset of my second year at the College School, I became the official *atelierista* instead of one of the co-teachers in the 4- and 5-year-old preschool classroom. This was a great relief to me. I finally had the freedom and the responsibility to concentrate on what I had come to do—help teachers and children to learn more about and to use language, the visual arts, and the practice of dialogue in increasingly rich and satisfying ways.

In addition, my new position gave me the opportunity to move ahead with last year's preschool class and to begin to do some work with them as kindergartners. I wanted to continue to work with these children and their already keen interest in plants. It was my hope to follow a small group of children through a continuation of the Garden Project, looking closely at their conversations and their ideas in writing, drawing, and clay. By following a particular group of children over time, I hoped to learn more about the relationship between their work in these symbolic media and their emerging understanding of and feeling for the plant world. I remembered the close relationship and sophisticated understanding of the seasonal stages of Mil, the adopted apple tree at the Diana School, which the children had expressed in language, drawings, and clay. I hoped that these kindergarten children might have a similar experience with the plants that they would come to know.

Honey Norlander and Kathy Seibel, the kindergarten teachers at the time, agreed to work with me. They liked the idea of continuing the Garden Project and suggested that it would work best for them if we included the whole class. We met several times in June 1993 to discuss possible ways to continue the project. I knew of a program in Vermont called Foodworks, which I wanted to investigate. Kathy knew of a curriculum by the National Gardening Association, which she agreed to research. We left for the summer prepared to inform ourselves about gardening in early childhood education and to look for resources that might be useful for us.

During these meetings, we also decided that I would begin working with the entire group, but that I would carefully observe and collect the comments, writing, and drawings of seven children in particular. We discussed the possibility that I might continue to work with the small group in the spring if they felt the whole class was ready to move on to some other topic.

Kathy and Honey suggested that we work on this project during their "theme time," which was scheduled twice a week for an hour-and-a-half period. We suspected that the project might last between 8 and 12 weeks. The kindergarten teachers had many of their own curriculum goals and plans, some of which had been developed at the College School. They, therefore, had limited time to give to the project during the school day.

There was clearly less flexibility in the kindergarten than there was in the preschool at the College School and certainly far less than there had been in Reggio Emilia, where a project often becomes the entire focus for children and their teachers.

In spite of the time limitation, the three of us had agreed that instead of following the predetermined plans of a teacher-managed theme, we would build this project with children. This departure from the standard practice of following a set curriculum has been well articulated by my colleague, Brenda Fyfe (1995).

> This way of working with children does not rely on a set of fixed curriculum goals and objectives with a prescribed or highly recommended set of learning activities. Instead, emergent, negotiated curriculum is guided by teachers' goals and values, an understanding of child development, and on-going observation and study of children. It is co-constructed by children, teachers and parents. It requires that children's minds are engaged, and above all, it requires great respect for the ideas, questions, feelings, capabilities and interests of children.

Practically speaking, this approach requires teachers to arrange for and use small-group conversations and extensive visual languages as the curriculum core. It demands time to meet and discuss children's work in order to decide how to go forward. We faced the challenges of learning more about these practices in the midst of our work together, as we did, and still do, in the preschool. This was not easy. Because of our busy schedules, it also seemed difficult to find time to meet together to review children's work and to plan possible next steps.

Because of these limitations, what developed out of our work together is not an example of a skillfully orchestrated project like the many from Reggio Emilia. It was more a series of experiences with children and plants, some of which were more successful than others. However, because I continued to work with my small group of children and their parents for an additional 5 weeks in the spring and throughout the summer, the series of experiences began to take on more meaning for those of us who were involved for a more extended period of time.

Kathy, Honey, and I met again in the fall. We decided to begin our work together sometime early in the second semester of the next year. We also decided to select together the children who would compose the small group.

Kathy and Honey helped me choose a balanced group of boys and girls with a variety of strengths who would work well together and who showed particular interest in the subject. The group we chose included Dan, Jessica, and Milla, who had been in preschool with me, and Evan, Adam, Katie, and Kateri, who were joining the class for the first time.

In the following sections of this chapter I will discuss some of the highlights of the Garden Project as it emerged for the whole kindergarten class, and the group of seven children in particular, including the first conversations about seeds and plants with the class, the children's designs and plans for a classroom grow table, their journals in which they followed the growth of beans, and clay "portraits" of plants. In each case, I will discuss several examples of children's work in depth.

Beginning with Conversations

When the kindergarten teachers and I reviewed possibilities for continuing the Garden Project, we noted that both Foodworks and the National Gardening Association had written and built curricula around grow tables in the classroom. This seemed like an exciting possibility to us. However, we had learned from Reggio Emilia that it is critically important to involve children in the direction of a project right from the beginning. According to the educators in Reggio Emilia, in a good project there should be many opportunities for children and teachers to share ideas or, as we saw in the Tree Project, to pass them back and forth like a ball in play.

I had observed the first conversation of a project called "The Amusement Park for the Birds" in Reggio Emilia during my internship at La Villetta School. It was led by Amelia Gambetti and included 11 children from the 5- and 6-year-old class. She initiated the conversation by asking the children what they remembered about what had been built in the park behind the school the year before. The children remembered many specific things about a bird observation station, bird feeders, and a little pond that the older children had made. Then, seemingly without any suggestion or indication from Amelia, they began elaborating on what else could be done to the park that would make it even more interesting for the birds.

This conversation led to an agreement between the teachers and the children to work on the construction of a more elaborate version of the bird park than the one that had been there the previous year, even to the extent of building an amusement park for the birds and other little animals. Although the project began with eleven 5- and 6-year-old children in February, by the spring all the children in the school were involved somehow in the creation of this fantastic park of fanciful fountains, waterwheels, and feeders.

Engaging in a group conversation seemed to be a good way for us to begin with the kindergarten at the College School as well. Because about half the kindergartners were new students and half were coming up from preschool at the College School, we decided not to focus right away on remembering the experience with plants from the previous year, but rather to begin by asking the group of kindergartners more generally what they knew, understood, remembered, and wondered about seeds and plants. We planned to have this discussion with the whole class. The following is a transcription of most of the conversation held in the morning on January 18, 1994:

Louise: What do any of you know about growing seeds? Have you planted seeds? What do you remember about seeds?

Sam: You dig them into the ground. You cover them up. You water them and then they will grow. You don't sing to it [the seed] . . . ahhh! [*singing in a high opera imitation voice*]. Or, you don't play to it, and you don't read to it. You just watch it, and then you grow it. You water it, you watch it, and then you grow it.

Louise: You don't need to sing to it or read to it?

Joe: You don't need to do anything.

Louise: And it will just grow?

Joe: You do need to water it.

Phillip: And, it needs sun, too.

Adam: Or, you can put a light over it.

Sam: (*Stands up and gestures*) If this is the sun, the circle that I'm making, and this is a plant, you keep it up to the sun and then you water it and it will grow. And if you water it too much, it will die and not grow. So, you don't want to *overwater* it.

Louise: So, you have to know just how much water it needs.

Sam: Because the bag, if you buy it in bags, tells you how much. The directions are on the back.

Adam: If you grow plants inside, you put it in dirt and you water it and you can put a light over it instead of sun.

Louise: So, sometimes you can grow plants with a light?

Adam: Yeah.

Joe: It happens!

Louise: I think I've seen that, too.

Katie: If it gets too much sun, then they'll die.

Joe: They need the right amount of water and sometimes they need the right amount of sun. We tried to grow pumpkins once and they didn't grow.

Louise: Why do you think they didn't grow?

Joe: Because they got too much water.

Shelly: Plants need air.

Louise: So, we've said they need sun, water. They also need air?

Kateri: Winter kills the plants.

Katie: You can bring them in. Then you can put them out in the spring.

Jessica: My dad can tell me about how plants grow.

Chelsey: Once I planted plants.

Joe: Seeds need water, sun, and air. Sometimes they can take all the day in the sunlight.

Sam: They always can.

Louise: But you said before it depends on what kind of plant.

Sam: Sometimes it does, but there are different kinds of brands, and they need different things.

Louise: Same seed, different brands?

Joe: There are different brands and some just appear from God's magic. Some
get down from trees.

Louise: Is that right? They don't all come in packages? Some of you last year
did some things with seeds. What do you remember about growing
seeds?

Several: The plant sale!

Phillip: I remember we planted seeds in the sand table and remember, I made
that banner.

Louise: You made a big banner. What did it say?

Phillip: It said, "Preschool Plant Sale."

Louise: That was your idea to make a great big sign, wasn't it?

Phillip: We planted seeds by the rock path in Dorris's room. And I also helped
with the money.

Eight out of 20 children spoke during this portion of the conversation.
Others listened to what those children said and some were uninterested and
fidgety. This is the nature of having a conversation of this length with this many
children. Most of the time, young children are better able to develop the ability
to focus and to contribute to a discussion in a smaller group. That is why most
conversations of length and depth in Reggio Emilia take place in a group of 5 to
12 children.

In reviewing this large-group conversation, it is clear that the children
who did participate were eager to share and exchange ideas and memories.
What did these children know, understand, remember, and wonder about plants
in this conversation?

Sam begins with a remarkable statement that sets the tone for the conversation—an enumeration of the subtle variations in the needs of plants. Sam
begins by declaring what plants do not need and perhaps implying what children
do need. I surmise he is saying that in order for a baby or a young child to grow,
it needs to be nurtured with singing, music, and stories. He speaks in a tone of
awe and admiration about the seed that just grows all by itself. You just have to
watch and wait and it will grow. He does slip in that you do water it, which is
soon reiterated by Joe.

When Phillip adds that the seeds need sun, Sam stands up to show with
his hands how the plant should be close to the sun to receive light. After the
mention of sun, Adam mentions twice that artificial light can be substituted to
grow plants inside.

What follows are more distinctions about what plants need—different
varieties need different amounts of water and light. All plants need air and
enough warmth, and they need to be in the ground. Some seeds come in packages, some from trees, and some from God's magic. The children end with some
memories of the preschool plant sale.

Like the conversation that initiated "The Amusement Park for the Birds,"
this one gave the children "the ball." It gave the adults the opportunity to listen
to the children's many ideas and to their delightful perspective. Since the idea
of growing plants "inside under a light" had been mentioned by Adam, it appeared to be something some children had heard of and might be excited about
trying.

We followed up the first conversation the same afternoon with a small group of children who wanted to continue the discussion and to think about ways we might continue to learn about plants. The following is an excerpt of the second discussion.

Louise: This morning we talked about all the things you knew about growing seeds. Now we'd like your ideas about what things we could do this year if we want to continue to learn about seeds and plants?

David: I think we could do another sale. I'd definitely like to do it again because my plant died right away. I can't even raise a plant.

Louise: You'd like to know how to raise a plant?

Sam: I know how to. I could help him learn.

David: My mom is a good gardener.

Joe: Me, my mom, my dad—we are all good at it.

Louise: Someone talked this morning about growing plants under special lights. That's something we didn't do last year. What are some other ideas you have if we want to continue a project about plants?

Milla: Last year Nancy knew a lot about plants. We could ask her.

Louise: So, we could ask people to come in who know about plants.

Milla: Jessica's dad knows a lot about plants. Her father owns a greenhouse.

Louise: What are other possible ideas? We might want to have a special place to grow plants with lights. We could ask people to come help us who know about plants. Maybe we could make more of a greenhouse than we did last year.

Evan: That's too big a project. You need major bucks for that.

Joe: You just need lots of money, but not major.

Louise: We do have some money. We have about $60.

Adam: We could buy all we needed to make a plan for plants for $60.

Louise: Is your idea to spend the money from last year to grow plants inside? If you did, what plants would you want to grow? Would you want to grow things you could eat? Flowers? Herbs?

Ariel: I want to grow flowers. My favorite is the broken heart flower. I also want to grow lettuce and radishes.

Joe: One thing you shouldn't grow inside is pumpkins.

Designing the Grow Table

We all decided, teachers and children together, that we would like to design a grow table for the kindergarten classroom. We had collected various plans from the National Gardening Association, but we wanted to toss the ball back to the children. We hoped that they would want to envision and design this special table. We suggested that we work in two groups. By choice, one group worked with Kathy to determine the dimensions of the table. The rest of the group chose to work with Honey and me to invent possible grow table designs.

The group that worked on measurement chose to begin with unifix cubes. The table needed to fit in a particular place in the classroom, so the length was measured in cubes. The children still needed to determine the height and width. After much deliberation, they decided that the table should be low enough for

Benjamin, the shortest member of the class, and the width of two of their arm lengths put together so they all would be able to reach to the middle of the table. Katie, who knew quite a bit about measuring, brought in her grandfather's tape measure and translated the unifix cube measures into feet and inches. This process took three sessions of approximately one hour each. In the end, the children had determined dimensions that would fit in a specific space and be tailored to their size.

After having discussed it together, Honey and I suggested to the children in our group that they work in pairs to draw their grow table designs. Many children liked this idea and agreed to try. I remembered the rich work that grew out of children working together in pairs and small groups at the Diana School. I hoped that these children would both enjoy and stretch each other's ideas and imaginations through working together.

The children chose between 5 × 10 inch heavy white paper and 9 × 18 inch standard drawing paper. They chose among a variety of black drawing pens and the soft, colored pencils for their drawings. Reading from our notes of their comments, we reminded them of all the things they had said that plants need to grow—the right amount of water, sun or a grow light, soil, and air. We asked them to see if they could design a table taking all these needs into consideration.

The inventive drawings that began to emerge caught us by surprise. We did not expect the range and diversity of solutions, the wild and elaborate ideas for water, light, and soil systems, or the complexity of the drawings. It was as if the children had entered an architectural design collaboration. They were eager and fascinated to see what solutions other children had invented.

Four Grow Table Designs

What follows are the designs and accompanying explanations of Kateri, Adam, Jessica, and Milla, four of the seven in my small group. I have chosen to discuss the work of these four children as they offer the clearest examples of invention and expression of wonderful ideas through the medium of drawing. Kateri drew her table by herself, the other three chose to work in pairs with other children in the class: Adam with Alex, Jessica with Elysia, and Milla with Ariel. Both the designs and explanations of these children are the result of the collaboration of two children and must be viewed as such.

Kateri seemed confident in her ability to draw her ideas and was eager to begin (see Plate 5). In her simple line drawing, she used a combination of horizontal, vertical, curved, and circular black lines and dots to draw her table and the system that provides for the plants. She used colored pencils to decorate the plant pots, the hanging watering cans, and lights. Her system works by providing artificial light, water from watering cans, and soil that sprinkles down from boxes on the top rod. She drew arrows to indicate that the rods move back and forth so that all the plants will receive these three necessary things. It seems logical to Kateri to stack up the plants' three needs—light, water, and soil—which she has reviewed with her classmates. She lines them up in order, right above the plants. The lightness and daintiness of this drawing, as well as its movement and the play of the lines and the color choices, are reminiscent of Paul Klee's twittering machines. Kateri offered this explanation of her design:

The lights are attached to the first rod, the watering cans to the second, and the soil sprinkles down from high boxes on the third rod. The rods are attached to the wall. They move back and forth.

Adam and Alex are best friends. They were pleased to have the chance to collaborate and began by discussing their ideas together (see Figure 6.1). Where did they get the idea of a double-decker grow table? Perhaps they both wanted to draw one level, perhaps they liked the idea of bunk beds, perhaps they were thinking of plants on a series of shelves in a window. Unfortunately, I never asked them what inspired their wonderful idea. In their design, each plant has its own light, which looks something like a contemporary bedside lamp. The boys told me later that the orange dots in the middle of the yellow lights contained a special substance to keep the bugs away. They explained to me that the showers can rotate to water plants outside the grow table or to water the plants inside the grow table. They, like Kateri, have the idea that the soil, which the plants also need, will be supplied from the boxes on the tops of each grow table deck. When I asked what the green, yellow, and blue colored lines inside the table were, they told me they were like wallpaper—a final decorative touch. The boys decided together what features to include and how they would represent each one. Each boy drew some of each part of the drawing. Adam and Alex described their design in this way:

> This is a double-decker grow table design. Each plant has a light. Water comes from the showers and soil from the boxes. We added the colors to be like wallpaper.

FIGURE 6.1.   Adam and Alex's Grow Table Design

FIGURE 6.2. Jessica and Elysia's Grow Table Design

Like Adam and Alex, Jessica and Elysia are good friends. They play together and draw together often. They are excited to have the shared responsibility of creating a grow table design (see Figure 6.2). Jessica has spent many hours playing in her family's commercial greenhouse. She undoubtedly has noticed some of its features. Together, the two girls have included many features that have not appeared in other drawings—a transparent table, worms in the soil, a large heater, as well as a light source, a water system in the ceiling, switches for operating the systems, a window with slats to let in sun and fresh air, and, finally, a watering can in case the system fails. They also have planted carrots right in the soil of the table instead of envisioning plants only in pots. They have kept the soil in the table—it does not sprinkle down from above, for Jessica is probably too experienced in horticulture to come up with this theory.

This drawing seems to come alive. One can almost see the worms wiggling and feel the water pelting down on the carrots, the heat of the great hanging lamp, and the fresh air and sunlight coming through the tiny window. The girls have made expressive and energetic marks with both the pens and the colored pencils. Jessica drew with this same confidence and energy in preschool and will continue into first grade. Today, she shares her energy with Elysia, who is usually more delicate in her approach. Elysia is thrilled with the results and seems happy to have ventured into new expressive territory with this collaboration. This is how the two girls describe their grow table:

You can see through the grow table to see the soil and the worms. The worms help the plants get dirt. They help keep the plants healthy. There is a switch to turn on the large heater and light over the table. The switch turns on the water, too. There is a water system in the ceiling. The watering can is for when the switch is broken. There are slats in the window to let in fresh air and sun.

Milla and Ariel both have strong ideas. After they drew the table structure together, each girl worked on one side of the drawing as they talked together about what to include (see Figure 6.3). These girls decided to include some of the features found in other designs—individual lights, soil sprinkling boxes, and a water sprinkler. Unlike the other children, they indicated a water source—the sink. There are two sinks, one for each side of the table. Both girls wanted to draw one and perhaps they like the symmetry it gives to their drawing. To Ariel, the round shapes on the top left are lights. She chose to color them orange to indicate the heat and light coming from them. She says the cloud-like shapes are a kind of cotton to protect the plants from too much light. The girls have included letters and arrows to label parts in their drawing—"Sbeglr" is sprinkler, "Sgk" is sink. Another interesting feature is the recycling system, which holds surplus water and soil as mud that later dries out, and is reused in the table. They explained how their design functioned using these words:

The dirt, light, and water are attached to a pole. The sprinkler system is attached to tubes attached to the sink. If there is too much dirt or wa-

FIGURE 6.3. Milla and Ariel's Grow Table Design

ter, it runs off to the container under the table. The dirty water runs off to mud at the bottom and becomes dirt to recycle.

Revisiting the Grow Table in First Grade: Milla's Second Design

As I mentioned in the beginning of this chapter, the Garden Project continued into the summer between kindergarten and first grade for the group of seven children through planting, caring for, and harvesting a summer garden with their parents and the first-grade teacher. As the small group shared their experience with the whole class, the other children's interest in the Garden Project was renewed. During the process of remembering and reflecting on the Garden Project in the fall of 1994, a group of children became particularly animated when they remembered their grow table designs. A group of three or four of these first-grade children became so excited just thinking about the systems they had invented, that they asked if they could please do it again. They remembered very specific details about what they had drawn and invented in kindergarten, and they now had new ideas to incorporate into the grow table systems. Milla's description of her second grow table, which she designed in the fall of her first-grade year, follows:

> I drew the little watering cans on the side. They hang so they are tipped. When you fill them up they, they sprinkle water. The water has special stuff in it that is food for the plants. There are little sprinkles. So it is light when it falls on the soil, and it just absorbs. The water coming from the watering cans on top is heavier than the water in the cans below. The drops are bigger and heavier. They don't all absorb. The extra sinks down to the water collector underneath. You know how water works in a sandbox. Some absorbs and some just sinks to the bottom. See the little black lines underneath the table. The water gets cleaned in between those lines. Then it is pushed back up to the top watering cans in a tube with a pusher that works like a spring. Boing! It's kind of like a circle. The tube goes outside underground. The worms crawl inside to the grow table through the tube. You can see through it and sometimes you can see the worms. [see Plate 6]

Milla's new drawing emerged from a combination of her past experience and her new ideas. It represents an integration of her memory of the table that actually was constructed, her memory of other children's design ideas from last year that had just been reviewed, the ideas from last year that she liked, and new inventions related to more complex ideas that she has this year in first grade. The drawing holds a marvelous collection of theories about water drops and rain, reflection and color, liquid fertilizer and absorption, water purification and worms. The drawing is charming in its delicacy and sophisticated in its complexity.

Like all these children, Milla has learned that drawings can hold whole, integrated systems of ideas that relate to each other. She knows from experience that drawings have the power to communicate these complexities to others. She knows that she can use the drawing materials in logical and fanciful ways, and that she can invent as many ideas to include in this system as she has the imagination and desire to pursue.

All these children have been captivated by the process of invention and by the challenge and fun of playing with many ideas at the same time—like a juggler with several balls in the air. They have thought about the plants' needs within the context of a system, not as single elements. They have shared, traded, and combined ideas. During their work together, they probably have become more interested in plants and their needs than most children their age. Quite possibly, they have also understood and expressed much more about conditions for growth through their own inquiry and inventions than any book or teacher could ever tell them.

In her book *The Having of Wonderful Ideas*, Eleanor Duckworth (1995) writes:

> The having of wonderful ideas is what I consider the essence of intellectual development. And I consider it the essence of pedagogy to give [children] the occasion to have [them]. . . . There are two aspects to providing occasions for wonderful ideas. One is being willing to accept children's ideas. The other is providing a setting that suggests wonderful ideas to children—different ideas to different children—as they are caught up in intellectual problems that are real to them. (pp. 1, 7)

The grow table sequence provides stunning examples of children's wonderful ideas that they have communicated through their drawings and their words. As teachers, we not only accepted their ideas, we asked for them. They knew how to use pens, paper, and colored pencils with ease. They knew that they could trust both their skill in the use of the materials and the medium of drawing to hold all their wonderful ideas and to communicate them to others. The next step was to honor the children's wonderful ideas by using them to build a functioning grow table for the classroom.

Building the Grow Table

Soon after the designs were completed, we put all the kindergarten children's drawings up on a bulletin board outside the classroom so that the children, their parents, and other members of the school community could admire them and discuss them. During the next phase of the project, teachers and children decided together which ideas might be incorporated into the actual table—it would be the dimensions that the children had decided on, it would be on wheels so it could be easily moved, it would have a transparent insert, and it would have a large grow light that would hang from double chains above it. Maybe it could have a water system with tubes. (I would like to note at this point that I would have liked to incorporate many more of the children's ideas into the table. However, because of limited time and the other constraints mentioned above, we were unable to.)

We asked parents and Dan, the maintenance man whom the children knew to be good carpenter, to help us build the table. With parents' and children's help we assembled the materials as the day for building arrived. All the children in the class watched with interest when the power tools were in use and took turns holding lumber and securing screws when it was safe for them to help. They all helped bring the table to its upright position as children and adults cheered. It was like an old-fashioned barn raising! All the children helped to sand the rough edges of the table once it was completed.

Jessica's father had offered to make the transparent insert for the base of the table, which Jessica and Elysia had designed. During the week we waited for the insert, we asked children what they would like to plant. We looked through seed catalogues and visited our favorite nursery. When the day for planting came, we filled the table with soil from the greenhouse and sowed lettuces, spinach, peas and sweet peas, green beans, and herbs.

Growing Beans, Keeping Journals

At the same time the table was planted, Kathy offered the children the chance to observe the growth from seed of their own individual pea or bean plant by planting it in a jar with cotton batting instead of soil. She also suggested that they record the growth they observed by keeping a "Bean Journal" in which they could draw, write, and measure what they noticed as the bean grew. She planned to be available several times a week to help small groups with measuring and writing.

This would be these children's first opportunity to keep a journal, and we were eager to see how the journals would develop. We wanted to know if the growth of a bean would hold the children's attention over time and if it would motivate them to write. We were equally curious to see how their drawings would progress. These drawings would be different than the grow table designs. Instead of coming out of invention and integration of imagined possibilities for a workable system, these drawings would come "from life" through the observation of a growing plant.

Two Children's Journals

I will discuss the bean journals of Dan and Adam as representative examples of the work of many children in the class and of the seven children in particular. Similar to most children's journals, they both show a progression from very simple, small drawings in pencil or pen only, to larger, quite complex pen and colored pencil drawings. The two examples are exceptional in that the two boys chose to draw, write, and measure in practically every entry. Both of them also chose to do clay "portraits" of their plants later in the spring. The pages of the journals that are reproduced here are greatly reduced. Each original drawing is on 8.5 × 11 inch paper.

Dan begins his journal with a small, one-inch pencil line drawing of his jar with its tiny bean drawn fairly indistinctly (see Figure 6.4). He records simply, "Bean planted on 3/1." On the second day, his bean drawing is more distinct and he notices that skin has come off. On the fifth day, the small jar triples in size, he includes many lines close together to represent the cotton behind the bean, and he draws and writes that "a root has sprouted." He chooses a pen instead of a pencil, perhaps to make a more definite statement. On the eighth day, he notices that the big root has sprouted a smaller one and he measures the root.

FIGURE 6.4.   Dan's Bean Journal, Days 1–8

Because of spring break, we skip to day 22 when Dan draws the many roots that have grown and writes about them (see Figure 6.5). He begins to use yellow and green colored pencils. As the plant grows, his drawings become much more lively and expressive. As he notices more, he becomes more and more excited about the transformation that is occurring.

On day 36 Dan fills the whole page with his drawing. His drawings are growing in stature, along with the bean. He notices and draws the heart-shaped leaves and measures his plant in centimeters. On day 63, he proudly draws and

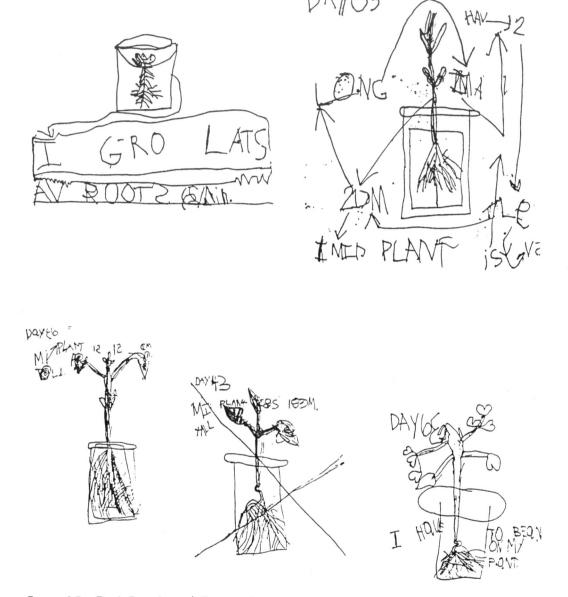

FIGURE 6.5. Dan's Bean Journal, Days 22–36

announces in his most clear writing that his plant has two beans! He has used inventive spelling until this day, when he asks Kathy to help him with standard spelling. He doesn't want anyone to miss the news about the beans.

Adam begins his journal with a pencil drawing similar to, but larger than, Dan's, with a distinct, shaded bean in the middle of the jar (see Figure 6.6). He writes, ''Bean Planted 3/2/94.'' On the second and fifth days, he makes similar

FIGURE 6.6. Adam's Bean Journal, Days 1–32

drawings and writes, "no change." On the eighth day he discovers a "hole" in his bean, which he records in writing. Day 23 is an exciting one, after the return from spring break, for Adam discovers, writes about, and draws his plant, which has sprouted roots and three leaves. He has chosen to draw with pencil until this day, when he chooses to draw and write in yellow and purple colored pencils, perhaps in celebration of the birth of leaves and roots.

On day 32, he writes that his plant has "sprouted taller," and he measures it at 8 inches. He draws twin leaves at the top of the plant and uses crosshatch marks to fill them in, perhaps to indicate the veins of the leaf.

On day 36 Adam pays more attention to the wiggliness and the length of the roots and wiggles his pen to imitate the roots in his drawing (see Figure 6.7). He draws the symmetrical leaves a little larger than in the last drawing. He chooses dark-green colored pencil for the leaves, yellow for the jar, and brown for the small part of the seed remaining on the stem, which he has noticed and included in both of his last drawings. He uses color in most of the rest of his drawings.

On day 44, Adam makes three attempts to draw his plant the way he wants to, the last one representing the three pairs of leaves and the wiggly roots. He also uses two pages from now on to draw his bean, which has gotten so tall that he can't seem to fit it on one page. On day 51, he is so excited about the discovery of a flower on his bean plant that he spills water from the jar on his drawing. He exclaims in writing that his "plant has a flower on the tip!"

Day 64 brings the excitement of a bean and, as in Dan's journal, a clear declaration that "my plant has a big bean!" Adam draws the bean with large dots inside to represent the new bean seeds inside.

In his last drawing, he writes that his plant has lost all its leaves. He uses only a single line to represent his once flourishing bean plant.

The Value in Keeping a Journal

These boys and the other children have learned a great deal from the experience of keeping the bean journal. To begin with, because they have been invited to study the process of transformation over time, they have paid very close attention to each change. They seemed especially attentive because the beans belonged to them. They took ownership and pride in the plants' growth, like parents. In this sense, their sentiments are similar to those of the children of Reggio Emilia who adopted a tree. Although they did not keep journals, the Italian children noticed the subtle changes in Mil, the apple tree, during the spring months. Like Adam, they noticed that the fruit grows from the flower. Perhaps the 5- and 6-year-old children in both Reggio Emilia and St. Louis were aware of these subtle changes because they had an emotional attachment to the tree or the plant, visited it often, and were as curious and attentive to the changes as they might be to a new haircut or the lost tooth of a friend.

The kindergarten children probably would not have noticed the detail of the structure of each part of the plant as it grew if they had not been drawing it. I had suggested the technique of contour drawing, or "bug drawing" as it often is called. By pretending that they were watching a tiny insect crawling slowly over the contour lines that defined the stem, the roots, and the new leaves, they were able to follow the path of the imaginary insect with both their eyes and

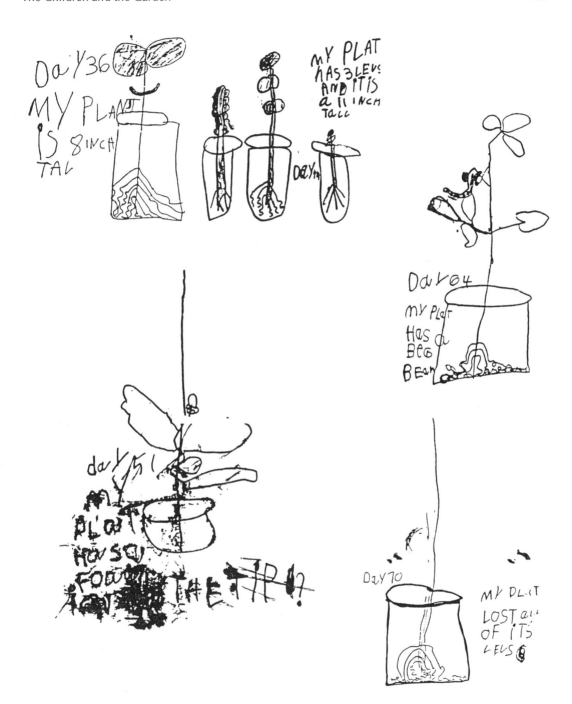

FIGURE 6.7. Adam's Bean Journal, Days 36–70

their pens. This approach to seeing and drawing offers to both children and adults an interesting, fanciful way to notice more.

The idea of writing, drawing, and measuring in one place about one thing was both exciting and grounding for these children, whose experience in school is sometimes fragmented. They were able not only to put many of their developing skills to use in a way that interested them, but also to stretch themselves and increase their ability and confidence in these skills over the 60 or 70 days of the beans' growth. Their skills, their excitement, and their pleasure in keeping their journals grew as their beans grew.

During this time, these children learned about the discipline required to keep an observational sketchbook/journal and about the satisfaction it provides. This time-honored practice of naturalists, writers, and artists offers a way to observe phenomena closely and, at the same time, to let the mind respond and play with images and ideas. It often is used as a source for later, more developed, polished work. Most of the teachers at the College School give the journal and sketchbook/journal a prominent place in their curriculum. These children will continue this practice in school.

One alternative for the kindergarten children would have been to share beans and perhaps bean journals. Perhaps they would have shared more collective excitement in friendship during the bean growing. No doubt, they also would have shared skills—learned from each other's drawing styles—and helped one another with writing and measuring. Perhaps they would have been less dependent on a teacher for help in measuring and writing if they had worked alongside a more able friend.

I think specifically of the grow table collaborations that happened this year and the many collaborative efforts of children that I witnessed in Reggio Emilia. It appears that children who work together to consider questions that are interesting to them, in the right setting, with familiar materials, often have even more wonderful ideas than they do when working independently. They seem to learn from each other through sharing their unique skills, perspectives, and styles of working and communicating.

Sculpting Ideas with Clay

Toward the end of April, I offered the seven children the choice to come into the *atelier* to work with clay. I suggested that they might want to represent some of their ideas about plants using a sculptural, three-dimensional medium. The children who were most interested in this idea were Dan, Adam, and Evan. Dan and Adam were both thrilled with the idea of making a clay relief "portrait" of their bean plants. They brought their bean journals to the *atelier* to refer to, as well as the full-grown bean plants themselves. Evan wanted to make a standing sculpture of tulips that he had drawn on a class field trip to the Missouri Botanical Garden. The three boys worked at the same table during three different one-hour sessions over a period of 10 days. For the most part, they worked independently, asking me for tools and technical help when needed. They were each interested in what the others were doing but at the same time keenly concentrated on their own work. Each boy seemed to have a clear idea in mind of what he wanted to do.

I realized that I could have suggested that they work together. Somehow in this case, I had the feeling that they needed to work on their own pieces. This was their first opportunity during the year to work with clay in the *atelier*, and I thought that this time they needed the chance to work out their own ideas and their own way with the clay. It would have been ideal to follow the individual work with a collaborative sculpture, but the constraints of time did not allow it. What follows is a description of their work.

The Bean Portraits

Dan and Adam and I discussed possible formats for their clay work, just as in Reggio Emilia Marco, Bobo, and their teacher Marina Mori had decided together on the best choice for a format for their sculpture of the tree "taking in the bad air and spitting out the good air." We chose relief sculpture because it would be difficult to sculpt a spindly bean plant that would stand upright.

We rolled half-inch slabs together. After that, they decided what shape and size slab they wanted to work on. They both cut rectangular slabs of about 8 × 12 inches. Although Dan had more experience with clay in preschool than Adam, both boys had made slab dinosaurs in the art room in conjunction with a fall classroom theme. They were both familiar with the techniques of building up on the slab with additional pieces of clay, incising into it with a variety of tools, and imprinting with fingers or found objects. They both knew how to use slip as glue to hold pieces of clay together.

Dan had decided earlier that he wanted to make his bean using only coils. During the time he was shaping the clay, he referred to the last page of his journal and to the bean plant often. He wanted it to be a good likeness, a true portrait of his bean in full maturity. He carefully formed the heart-shaped leaves out of the coils and added small cross pieces to represent the veins. He made sure he had included the right number of leaves on each stem. He added his two clay coil beans. He shaped the roots as he observed them to be, with more attention than he had in his journal drawings. He chose not to include the jar (see Figure 6.8).

When it came time to choose ink colors to paint the bisque-fired clay, Dan chose two varieties of green for the plant, a blue background, and yellow for the roots. The coils turned out to be a good match for Dan's expressively solid pen lines and stocky drawings. He loved shaping the coils between his fingers and watching his clay portrait come to resemble his bean plant in more than two dimensions.

Instead of using coils to make his portrait, Adam decided to incise lines and use tools to imprint into his clay slab. Instead of using his journal as a reference, Adam used a pen drawing he had done of his bean plant. Like Dan, he wanted his clay portrait to be accurate. He wanted it to hold all he had discovered about how his bean plant grew. He began to draw all he knew with a fine-pointed clay tool—the fine root hairs, the stem with its bean seed still attached, and his fat bean. He wanted to include the sun in lines and bright yellow ink after the piece had been fired. He made both the rain drops and the bean seeds inside the bean by imprinting with the end of a paint brush. It was a lovely way to show that the rain and the seed are interconnected (see Plate 7).

The boys' bean portraits are a lasting testimony to their careful observations of the miracle of growth. The clay slab portraits hold all that they have

FIGURE 6.8. Dan's Bean Portrait

learned and also their great admiration and close feeling for these plants. They have shaped the details of the structure of the plants in their own individual expressive styles. The colors of water, sun, and earth and their brightness made the pieces sing. There are no borders or boundaries to their slabs. Somehow, they seem to be small pieces of the whole world of plants and sun and rain. They relate to our first conversation about seeds in January when children told us that plants need water, sun, and soil—that they do not need songs or stories, they just grow! The portraits remind me of Katie's statement in the conversation about fall leaves: "I know who does it; the wind and the rain and the clouds and the sun. God does it!" The boys' clay pieces have some of the same awe, wonder, and all-encompassing openness to the natural world as these children's words.

Evan's Sculpture

As part of the project on plants, the whole class had visited the Missouri Botanical Garden, which is known worldwide. It is innovatively designed on 79 acres of city land to include, among other plantings, an English woodland garden, a Japanese garden, a garden for the deaf and blind, and a huge domed climatron that houses a rain forest. The field trip was planned by the kindergarten teachers, who invited me to come along. While we were there, the children were encouraged to draw a plant or flower that they particularly liked. It was a beautiful April day, and the children spread out among the grape hyacinth, tulips, and pansies, all in glorious bloom.

I remember watching Evan and his mother, who was along as a helper that day, as they sat together in front of a bed of red tulips. Evan seemed reluctant to begin to draw, and his mother evidently was trying to counsel him. He did a drawing in the end, but he did not seem very pleased with it. Evan was particularly strong in math. While he helped enormously with counting the money from the plant sale and seemed quite interested in what we were doing with the Garden Project in other areas, he seemed to lack confidence in working with materials.

I was glad that Evan was eager to work with the clay along with Dan and Adam. Remembering the discouraging time he had at the Botanical Garden, I was also somewhat surprised when he said that he would like to sculpt the tulips. He wanted to bring his drawing of the tulip with him to the *atelier* and he seemed sure that he wanted to make a three-dimensional sculpture. He said he wanted to work on a slab, but that he would build up from it. He cut out a round piece of slab about 10 inches in diameter. He then made a very fat coil, which he stood up on end and attached to the slab with slip. Next, he began to flatten balls of clay into pancake-like pieces, which he added to the top of the vertical coil (Figure 6.9).

After edging the flat round piece with small bits of clay, he began to add little upright coils in the middle of his flower to represent the stamens he had noticed and drawn inside the tulip. This was a monolithic flower! Evan was very pleased with it. He decided to make more, so he began the process over again. When he was finished, he had made five tulips and a bee, which was balanced precariously on the edge of one flower. "The bee is pollinating the flowers," Evan explained. He used a looped tool to make a texture on the slab for grass.

FIGURE 6.9. Evan's Tulips

When he began to paint the fired piece, he chose red for the tulips, yellow for the pollen, and a light green for the grass.

I had never seen Evan so satisfied and pleased. I had the feeling that he finally had made the statement that he wanted to make about the tulips and about himself. He had been frustrated with the two dimensionality of drawing. The clay offered him the freedom to give form to what he knew and what he imagined. The tulips were more like a grove of trees than a bed of flowers—solid and strong, yet lyrical at the same time. This monumental style is similar to the work of several twentieth-century artists like Henry Moore and Fernand Leger who exaggerated the weight of forms in their work. The effect is bold and impressive.

The clay gave the three boys another way both to discover and express their concrete knowledge of plants and to give form to their growing feeling of "connectedness" with plants. The clay connected them naturally to the earth—it smells fresh, musty, and cool. They could shape and form it between their fingers, flatten it with their palms, imprint it with their fingernails. It is a sensuous, malleable medium. With the clay, the boys gave shape and form to their ideas, while at the same time the boys were shaped and formed by what they made. Their clay pieces reflect what they have come to understand and feel about these plants in their lives. Each piece is unique, as each child is. When they look at what they have made, they see the plants and at the same time they see themselves. What they have made and now hold represents a present relationship between each boy and his plant that was not clear before.

THE SUMMER GARDEN

By the end of April, most of the plants in the grow table had been sampled, transplanted, or taken home. We had hoped to prepare an outside garden at school for our grow table seedlings, but because of previous experience with vandalism, we decided against it. When Kathy's request to use a school neighbor's yard for a class garden was declined, the kindergarten teachers decided to move on to a new theme. Because I felt that my work and the work of the children in my small group was not yet finished, I looked for another alternative.

Fortunately, Skylar Harman, the first-grade teacher, heard of my dilemma and very generously offered her backyard, which was only a few blocks from school. She was interested in carrying the Garden Project into the first grade and she liked the idea of having a summer garden in her yard tended by a group of incoming first graders.

I wrote to all the parents of the group, asking if they would be willing to participate with us in this new adventure. I explained that we would need to work together to till the garden, enrich the soil, plant the seeds, and care for the garden throughout the summer. I also explained that I hoped the children and the parents would keep summer garden journals. The parents were willing and enthusiastic.

During the month of May, the group of seven children, now called the "garden group," helped to plan the garden. Skylar told us that it could be about 8 × 12 feet. One day, I asked the children how big they thought that dimension was. Katie suggested we round up some rulers and line them up on the playground blacktop to see. Two children volunteered to gather rulers and returned with 12 rulers and a yardstick. Katie led the others in using these measures and their own feet to lay down two sides of a rectangle. The children told me the other sides would match.

Another day, we visited the garden site to pace off our plot and talk about what we would need to do to turn the grassy spot into a garden. Dan said we would need to till it, which he told us meant to "turn over" the soil. He said his father had a tiller and could bring it over. Jessica said we would need to add fertilizer to the soil and that her mother and father could bring soil with turkey poop and fertilizer from their greenhouse to add to the soil. She said that her parents also could bring vegetable plants, "probably tomato and zucchini," if the other children wanted to plant them. Milla said we would need garden tools and that she had tools and garden gloves, which she could bring. All the children volunteered to bring seeds.

We spent several sessions back at school planning what seeds the children would want to plant and how we would arrange them in the garden. They had many different ideas, all based on different reasons. Milla, Katie, and Dan wanted to plant sunflowers because they loved the big, yellow centers and they wanted flowers that would grow taller than they were. Jessica wanted to grow green beans because she loved to eat them out of the picking basket in the garden at her house. Dan wanted to plant tomatoes because he liked the spaghetti sauce that his mother made from them in his home garden. Katie and Kateri wanted to plant carrots because they loved carrot sticks and they were sure carrots would help them to see well. Evan and Adam wanted to plant pumpkins so they would be able to make jack-o-lanterns at Halloween. The excitement was building.

We planned two different garden tilling and planting days at the end of May. Dan's father brought his power tiller, and Jessica's mother brought peat and lots of fertilizer. Milla brought her tools and gardening gloves. Everyone brought seeds and plants. The children took turns planting new seedlings, sowing seeds in the rich soil, and watering with the nearby hose. Skylar provided lemonade and cookies. We finally had a garden!

Together, the parents, Skylar, and I coordinated parent/child garden work crews throughout the summer. We divided the group in half. Each group of children and their parents would come every other week for about an hour to work in the garden and to write and draw in their journals about whatever they wished. Hopefully, they would record the changes they noticed in the garden and the delights of summer shared with friends.

My family and I had planned to spend the summer in Vermont. In the second week in June, I would be leaving the garden and Skylar and the children and parents behind for the summer, hoping that the experience would be a good one and that I would learn about it through their journals when I returned. I was happy that the children could have the experience of planting and watching a real garden grow alongside their friends. I was grateful to Skylar for offering to oversee the garden and host the families. I was thankful that the parents were willing to support their children in this experience.

Preparing to Keep Garden Journals

The last week of school, the children and I prepared two garden journals for each family. For the journal covers, the children chose a favorite photograph of themselves at work during the project. We filled the journals with sturdy, blank white drawing paper. Then, we laminated the covers and put the journals together with three rings.

In our last conversation together at school, I asked the children their opinions on the value of keeping a journal.

Evan: This is just the way you keep a journal: You draw and you write.
Jessica: You can tell what a person saw by reading it and you see what it
looked like by looking at the pictures.
Dan: Sometimes you have to draw the same thing when you are drawing a
plant because it grows slowly.
Adam: By keeping bean journals we learned what happens when they grow,
how sprouts come out, and how leaves grow and how it makes a bean.

When asked if they thought their parents could keep a journal, most children said their parents wrote frequently. Some said their parents drew often. All said they thought they could help their parents draw. For instance, Katie said, "I'd say that to begin with they need to begin to think they draw well. My mom can draw but she just doesn't think she can."

I remembered the attention and care that the teachers at the Diana School had given to the communication with parents about the summer plant care project for the 5-year-old children and their parents. Accordingly, I sent the following letter home to parents with the two journals and the children's conversation about journals.

Dear Parents: May 24, 1994

Here are your journals, one for your child and one for you. You might find the following suggestions useful:

- All kindergarten children kept records of the growth of their bean or pea plant in journals. They are accustomed to drawing and then writing (using inventive spelling) about what they notice about plants. They developed this kind of practice with Kathy. I think if they see that you value this activity and that you want to do it too, they'll join you.
- If children are stuck, I suggest simple contour drawing or "bug drawing." Pretend you are a small insect crawling along the edge of each leaf and vine. Your pen follows the path of the insect and the path of your eye. Suggest drawing lines and textures with the pen and coloring in large spaces with the colored pencils.
- You, as parents, know your children better than any teacher. You are in the best position to notice what they are thinking and wondering about the plants, the natural world around them, and themselves in it. We, as teachers and parents, can encourage children to be detectives and to keep thinking and wondering.

You could use your journal to record what your children are thinking and wondering or some of the conversations you have with them. You could record what you wonder together. These observations would help me understand your children's thinking if you are willing to share them.

Again, I thank you all so very much for your involvement and interest in this project.

Sincerely,
Louise Cadwell, *Atelierista*

I have found such pleasure in keeping sketchbooks/journals myself and with my family. Especially while traveling and during our year in Italy, drawing and writing together became a way to slow down and truly enjoy a particular place, instead of rushing to try to take in too much or do too much. The practice required that we "make something" of an experience, reflect together, and learn to appreciate each other's unique voice and insight. In our fast-paced lives, we rarely seem to find the time to deeply appreciate each other or our experiences. Keeping family sketchbooks/journals has become one way my family has learned to do both. In the summer garden, I hoped that this group of parents and children might begin to enjoy the rewards of this practice as well.

The Harvest

When I returned to St. Louis in September 1994, I was eager to visit the garden and to read the journals. I found out that the garden had grown beautifully. It had produced peas and beans, tomatoes and carrots, zucchini and tall sunflowers. The children and parents had come weekly to water and measure, weed and pick, play and admire the fruits of the garden. Skylar and several parents had taken photographs. Most parents and children had used their journals for writing, drawing, and measuring, and had included garden photos (see Figures 6.10 and 6.11).

The journals are a collection of memories of moments. Together, the individual voices tell the story of how they lived with the garden and with each other during this particular summer in this particular place. Skylar's backyard garden became familiar, the community of parents and children grew together, the practice of noticing, writing, and drawing found a place in their busy summer lives.

I would like to conclude by discussing four particular journal entries, each written by one member of two different parent/child pairs. These entries represent four different responses to the garden and to the practice of journal

FIGURE 6.10.   Planting the Summer Garden

FIGURE 6.11.   Harvesting the Summer Garden

writing and drawing. They demonstrate the pleasure and insight that children and parents offer each other when they share this practice.

Dan and his Mother, Mary Ann

Dan is just learning to form letters with confidence and to hear the letters' sounds in words that he can write. He has learned to draw what he sees this year through his careful, bold line drawings of his beautiful bean plant emerging slowly from its small seed. Here, he fills the page with both of these powerful languages that he is learning. He draws tomatoes, round, full, and fat, a big one and little ones, cherry tomatoes rolling off the page (see Figure 6.12). He fills the form the black pen line has defined with red soft pencil, which spills out of the black lines. His small green pepper is a different form, balancing in between tomatoes with its straight and curved lines corresponding to the shape of the stem and the shape of the fruit.

His letters and words are wonderfully confident as he shouts "tomatos" in letters as round and big as the drawing and the fruit itself. The "peper" word is more diminutive and dignified, tucked up beside its mate in its proper place. All these lines, circles, and color smudges come together to express Dan's feeling for these luscious and delightful vegetables and his joy and sense of accomplishment in making something of them—something that will last and remind him of the vegetables and his growing capability in both writing and drawing.

FIGURE 6.12. Dan's Garden Journal

His mother, Mary Ann, is quietly supportive. She appreciates his effort. She admires his work. She draws her own impressions of the garden—delicate, dainty leaf and curling vine lines of the bean pole teepee and the tall, golden sunflower (see Figure 6.13). Her drawings are competent renderings. Dan, in turn, admires her work and feels proud of her drawings. He sees the bean and the sunflower in a different way now—a way that includes his mother's image of the bountiful bean. Mary Ann writes only what Dan says in a quote next to the sunflower. She records the way he sees the garden through his eyes—the flower is past his height, the tiny seed has produced a plant that has overtaken him in only several weeks. She now sees the garden a little differently through his eyes.

Jessica and Her Mother, Susan

Jessica's mother, Susan, is busy with three children and her family's greenhouse business. She makes an effort to come to this garden, even though she has her own garden to tend, because she knows it is important to Jessica as well as the other children and parents. Every time she comes, she takes the time to write about what she observes, about the growth and change in the garden, and about what the children do (see Figure 6.14).

beans

maryann marinec!

"If used to be up to here (chin) and now its up to here." (above head)

Dan 6-29-94

FIGURE 6.13. Mary Ann's Garden Journal

She talks to herself in her journal—she comments on the weather, she tells what she sees, she comments on what she sees, she asks questions, she is frank. She uses the journal to record her impressions of the mood of the day as well as more specific observations. Her drawings complement her words. She notices three types of leaves on three different plants. These are almost short-hand drawings that could be used to identify the leaves at a later time. This style of writing and practice of sketching comes from a long lineage of journal writers like Henry David Thoreau, who wrote *Walden* (1854/1962) based on journal entries, and Aldo Leopold, author of *A Sand County Almanac* (1949).

Jessica is pleased that her mother writes and draws in her journal. Like Dan, she is proud of her mother and her ability to write and draw. She wants to know what her mother is writing about and listens with interest.

Jessica, on the other hand, has her own ideas and her own way of using

*Its a really hot, humied night in the garden. Jessica
& Katie were in attendance. Our neighbor Joey also came
w/ us There were more amazing changes in the garden.
Cucumbers are growing, and alot of cherry tomatoes.
Why do cherry tomatoes grow in multiples of 2? Eggplants
are blooming. But as the harvest begins so does
alot of other work. - weeds are also abundant and
the sunflowers are full of bugs)*

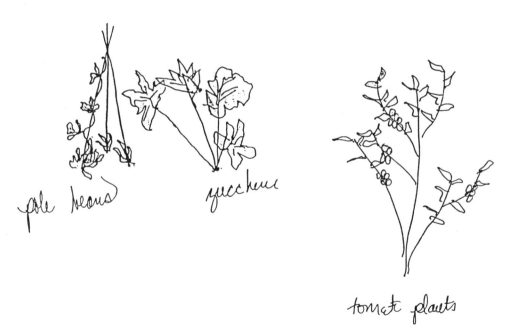

pole beans   zucchini

tomat plants

FIGURE 6.14.   Susan's Garden Journal

her journal. Although Jessica is very competent in writing for her age, she chooses not to write. She also chooses not to draw the growing vegetables, for she could do that as well with confidence and skill. She chooses, instead, to draw herself and her friend in the garden (see Figure 6.15). In the 3 years I have known Jessica I have noticed that she almost always includes herself in her drawings. She is interested in the social context around her and in placing herself in relationship to the important features of her world.

FIGURE 6.15. Jessica's Garden Journal

Here she has drawn a garden full of spontaneity and rhythm. Her drawing has the quality of what artists call a gesture drawing. Rather than the careful renderings of contour lines, the marks she has made capture the energy and motion of the subject. She and her friend have shovels in their hands, ready to dig. However, mostly they enjoy being in the middle of the garden and the trees. The two friends are caught in a moment in the garden, smiling and windblown, twins, like the two trees bowing on either side of the page. Bending arms and swaying bodies drawn in exuberant freedom are placed in an almost overlapping perspective. With this drawing, Jessica speaks in a joyous, bold, dynamic voice about her connection with the garden and her sense of place in it—alongside her friend. Her mother, her friends, and others can see and hear it clearly through "reading" her journal.

REFLECTING ON THE GARDEN A YEAR LATER

I was curious to know what the children would remember about our kindergarten Garden Project after a year's time. I wondered if the experiences with the seeds and plants and all the work with drawing, writing, and clay would have a lasting effect. In May 1995 I invited the children in two groups of two and one group of three to look at slides of the Garden Project with me and to talk about what seemed important to them about what and how we had learned together.

All seven of the children's responses are grouped with the questions that I asked in each small group.

Louise: You have told me how much you liked designing the grow tables. Can you explain to me why you liked it so much?

Milla: Well, it helped me think what was possible. It helped me understand what was possible. Also, what you can do and what was impossible.

Jessica: And, I had to think what a plant needs and what you would need to do if you weren't planting it in the table. I was thinking of what Mother Nature would do so I tried to make it like the grow table was Mother Nature.

Adam: I know the most fun thing was doing it with my best friend.

Katie: I just felt like doing something simple that day. I just did a table with a light on top of it.

Evan: Well, first you try to picture it and then . . .

Kateri: In your mind.

Evan: Yeah, in your mind and then you draw what you see there. Then they would have your idea about it and they might need your ideas to build it.

Louise: What did you like about putting some of your ideas in clay?

Dan: I have what I made at home, so I will remember about it for a long, long time. I will remember that I grew the seed. It's all in my journal.

Louise: What would someone looking at Adam's clay piece learn about plants?

Katie: That they are beautiful.

Adam: Well, I know how beans grow. First they start as a flower and then the little buds fall off and there's like a little bean inside a light blue circle and the little circle grows every day you water it. It gets bigger because it drinks more water and then, when it's ready, you eat it.

Katie: He put in rain drops and the roots.

Evan: The clay helps you remember. Models are three-dimensional and pictures are just flat. Models will make everything stand up.

Louise: What do you think writing and drawing in the journals helped you with?

Milla: Well, I always love drawing, so drawing the plants was like a treat. I know that they grow through the stages, and I learned that they were actually more interesting than I thought they were.

Katie: You remember when you did it, how you did it and everything, you know.

Evan: It helped us remember instead of pictures [photographs].

Adam: When you write about sunflowers, you think how big they are. When you draw them, you know how big they are.

Jessica: Drawing plants gives you more ideas of what they look like. I think it helps us because, well, if you forget all the stuff, you go find your journal and say, "I remember this."

Dan: I drew my bean lots of times. It started that small (*gesturing with his fingers*) and then it got bigger. It turned out to be as big as the jar. And we could measure them too.

Louise: Do you think it is important to learn about plants and seeds?

Milla: Well, plants are nature and it's all around the world. You need to learn about the world.

Jessica: You need to know how to take care of them because plants do have feelings and they might think, "This person that is taking care of me is too mean."

Adam: Because I found a tree in our backyard, and I never knew it was two hundred years old. And if you climb on their branches it's like their arms and if you peel off their bark, it's like their skin, and if a tree dies it's like us dying.

Katie: And especially you want to think about trees because trees give us lots of things like oxygen.

Louise: What are some of your favorite memories of the Garden Project?

Evan: I liked taking care of them. I mean, it's kinda nice. It gives you something to do in the summer.

Kateri: Taking care of little plants is just like holding a little baby. I remember when my mom drew me in the garden. She drew part of the garden. I loved that.

Adam: My favorite was when me and Katie built the tent for the beans and they grew up like Jack in the Beanstalk.

Katie: The pole beans jumped up them.

Adam: Yeah, and we called it Adam and Katie's Beanstalk.

Louise: Was it fun to grow a bean inside and then see how it would grow in the garden?

Adam: Yeah, it's different. The sun has more light and the sun is hotter and on a warm day it's better.

Katie: And on rainy days it gets more water.

Adam: Sometimes, you don't even have to water the plants outside because it rains a lot. I think they are happier outside.

Katie: Doing the garden was fun and it was learning.

Milla: As soon as it gets to be the hot season, then I think I want to go back to studying plants again.

I was pleased that the children had a collection of happy and vivid memories of our experiences together with plants. I was particularly interested, however, in the children's perceptions of how the materials helped them to learn. I was fascinated that designing the grow tables motivated Jessica to "think like Mother Nature," and Milla, Kateri, and Evan "to picture what was possible in our minds."

Thinking like "Mother Nature" brings to mind Aldo Leopold's (1949) essay, "Thinking Like a Mountain," where he describes the moment in which he awakened to an "ecological consciousness" through looking into the eyes of a dying wolf. This kind of "ecological thinking" requires both children and adults to take multiple perspectives and recognize the interconnected nature of all things.

In her book, *Children's Minds*, Margaret Donaldson (1979) cites many studies that show that children, indeed, do have the ability to take another's point of view, if they are able to do this within a context that is meaningful to them. Both the Tree Project at the Diana School and the Garden Project at the

College School offered children a rich and meaningful context in which they could identify with and "think like Mother Nature."

It was apparent through their comments that the opportunities both to draw and to work in clay helped the children notice and remember their ideas and their feelings of excitement about the bean plants, the grow table, and the summer garden. Dan says the details of the process of transformation of his bean from seed to vegetable is "all in my journal" and that through his journal and his clay piece, he will remember what he learned "for a long, long time." Evan says that, for him, the modeling in clay was most exciting "because clay makes everything stand up." The three dimensionality of the clay provided him with what was probably his first chance to embody all he knew and felt in a visual symbol.

Kateri says holding the plants is "just like holding a little baby." Jessica and Adam speak of how a plant would feel if harmed or ignored. They identify with the plants and attribute feelings to them. Rather than limiting their thinking to an egocentric perspective, this way of thinking contributes to their ability to identify with the plant world and to "think like a mountain." As Frank Winkler (1993) writes, it is one of the "treasures" that we need to carry with us over the bridge from childhood to adulthood.

Finally, the children loved the Garden Project. As Katie says, "Doing the garden was fun and it was learning." All the talk about and reflection on the Garden Project excites Milla to "want to go back to studying plants again," as she returned to designing a new and more complex grow table. Like the Tree Project at the Diana School, the Garden Project engaged children's minds over a long period of time. The many chapters of the project led them to new levels of understanding of complex processes through encounters with seeds and plants. The long story both supported and challenged them in finding form for their ideas and feelings in words, drawings, and clay, alongside their friends, their teachers, and their parents. The Garden Project helped them to build strong connections with the natural world. It led them to find a confident and sensitive voice, using language and making visual symbols to embody and express the relationships that they discovered with plants in the place that they had made called the summer garden.

This long story about children, teachers, plants, place, and parents confirms that, as adults, we need to nurture and support children's fundamental need to develop strong bonds with the natural world. We must help them find places to make their own worlds and we must find times together to dig in the soil, race with the wind, or gaze at the stars. As children and adults, we need wild places and we can often find them close to home. We need to share each other's sense of wonder. And together we need to reach for the language and participate in the making of symbols that will embody, hold, and communicate our experience for ourselves and for each other.

Epilogue

To attempt to adapt the principles and practices of the Reggio Approach in an American setting is a daunting task. In part, this is because the Reggio Approach is not a technique that can be reduced to specific steps to follow. Rather, it is a complex approach that has grown from the Italian educators' deep questions about the nature of the child and of education. When we began in St. Louis, we certainly did not understand the full implications of the changes in practice that we wanted to make.

At times, the complexity and depth of this approach to early education have seemed overwhelming. The approach is somewhat like the Buddhist image of "Indra's Net," a great web connected at the nodes by shining jewels which reflect all the rest of the net (Badiner, 1990). Indra's Net is a symbol for the interconnectedness of all creation. Similarly, every principle of the Reggio Approach has many threads and is connected to every other part of the whole.

To better understand the intricacy of this approach, it is helpful to observe that many of its principles are rooted in the Italian culture—some in the culture in general and some in the culture of the specific region of Italy where the city of Reggio Emilia is located. At the same time, however, it is also important to recognize that while these cultural elements and values have contributed to the construction and healthy growth of the Reggio Approach, they are not limited to Italians.

By way of concluding these stories about my journey to Reggio Emilia and back home again, I would like to discuss how the educators who work in the preschools of Reggio Emilia have chosen to construct an educational approach that is, in part, based on elements of their culture, in part, on deliberate choices that they have made, and, in part, on universal values which ring true all over the world. Throughout, I will suggest the major differences between our cultures and our approaches to early childhood education that we will need to address as American educators before we can adequately understand or attempt to implement aspects of the Reggio Approach in our own schools.

In terms of preprimary education, the first and most obvious difference between Italy and the United States is that preschool education and programs for children from birth to 6 is funded by the national and local government in every region of Italy. Care and education of infants, toddlers, and preschool children is a social service that the townships offer to families. The amount of money that cities and regions are able and willing to put toward this social and educational service varies.

In Reggio Emilia, the municipal government allocates 12% of its entire budget to fund the public preschools and infant/toddler centers (Department of Education, 1990). The public officials and the citizens of the town have made top-quality preschool education and child-care services one of their highest priorities. In the United States, though federal Head Start funds are available for programs that serve more than a certain percentage of low-income and at-risk families, and though some school districts provide funds for programs for preschool children, preschool education is not a government priority. In fact, recently, federal dollars for programs for young children have been cut.

A second important cultural difference is the way in which the Italians invest time and energy in social exchange. They find the time to discuss philosophical, psychological, cultural, and political issues wherever they are and in many contexts. Their conversations are not limited to their field or their own personal experience. The Italians seek to broaden the scope of discussions in which they engage and they are always eager to talk. They talk at meals, in the piazza, in meetings. The agenda is not planned minute to minute. There seems to be time to meander, reflect, and debate together about a number of ideas at once. This aspect of Italian culture is reflected in the lives and work of the educators in Reggio Emilia preschools.

This important cultural aspect also is reflected in the architecture of the towns and cities of Italy and in the buildings themselves. There is always a piazza or central square in the middle of town where people gather to talk and children to play. There are often courtyards in the center of apartment buildings for the same reason. The cafes or bars serve as places for extended conversation. I remember one of my Italian professors saying, "When something important happens, everyone goes to the piazza to celebrate or mourn or discuss the event."

The piazza or central halls of the preschools and the infant/toddler centers in Reggio Emilia imitate the central piazza of the towns. They are places to exchange ideas of all kinds with many different people. The interior courtyards and many windows of the schools not only let in the light, but also open to the world of experience and ideas outside the school.

A specific aspect of the culture of the region of Emilia Romagna and the area of north central Italy that builds on this fundamental aspect of Italian culture is their history of collaboration—through agricultural models of cooperative farms in particular. The preschools in Reggio Emilia were founded as a result of the efforts of groups of parents and the solidarity of the community. This history provides the foundation for the close partnership between parents and teachers and the basis for the emphasis on collaboration in learning and in teaching in the preschools of Reggio Emilia.

The historical foundation of collaboration supports the Italian educators' choice to adopt the co-constructivist view, which holds that we make sense of our experience and create our understanding of it through our interaction and close relationships with peers, mentors, materials, and ideas, rather than as isolated individuals.

In the United States, teachers often are secluded in solitary classrooms that become the individual teacher's turf. These teachers often find it difficult to make occasions to discuss and develop new ideas alongside other teachers. The discussions of teachers most often are limited to their field, education, and frequently are even more restricted to their own special expertise. American teachers do not cross disciplines as naturally and fluidly as the Italians do. In general, American teachers rarely take time in meetings or around a meal to linger over ideas, to debate, to bring our intellectual struggles to the table along-side our passionate feelings and intuitions.

American teachers do not often collaborate in the way that the educators in the preschools of Reggio Emilia have learned to collaborate with each other or with parents. Here, teachers are commonly the experts and parents become volunteers/helpers. Parents do not often receive the invitation or encouragement to contribute their voice to their children's education. In the United States, we place a great deal of importance on the individual, whether a child, teacher, or parent. The emphasis on the individual makes it difficult to shift our focus to include the picture of how individuals contribute to each other's growth and development. Adopting principles of the Reggio Approach means making this kind of shift.

Another aspect of Italian culture that the educators of Reggio Emilia value is the importance of beauty. Beauty is everywhere in Italy—in the architecture, the fabrics, the displays of fresh vegetables, fruits, and flowers. The pleasure that is taken in choosing materials, preparing and arranging the clothing one will wear, the food one will share at a meal, or the display one creates in a storefront, is apparent. This cultural aesthetic awareness permeates the preschools of Reggio Emilia. Every detail of the space is attended to. Each area is clean, orderly, full, and rich in natural and created objects. Each area is a delight to the eye. Photographs and written words of children and teachers are attractively displayed to clearly communicate the joy, significance, and depth of learning that takes place everyday in the schools.

In the United States, we have not placed much importance on beauty in schools. Often school architecture resembles that of a factory or mall, with long corridors, poor lighting, and institutional colors. Bright plastic toys, play structures, commercially made classroom decorations, and clutter often take over the space in many preschools. Adopting the Reggio Approach means rethinking the design of and attention we give to space and the materials we use in schools.

One aspect of the Reggio Approach that does not grow directly out of the culture is the image that the Reggio educators hold of a strong, capable, prepared child. In general, Italian children are overprotected. They are loved and cared for by the whole community. Certainly, it is agreed that children deserve the very best, but sometimes this means that things are done for them by adults.

In the Reggio Emilia preschools, however, each child is viewed as infinitely capable, creative, and intelligent. The job of the teachers is to support these qualities and to challenge children in appropriate ways so that they develop fully. The way in which the children in the Reggio schools are empowered both to use their natural curiosity and desire to discover more and more about themselves and their world and to engage their full imaginative and creative abilities is exemplary. We can learn from the Reggio educators to look at children differently, to expect more of them and of ourselves, and to offer them many more possibilities for full development.

All these ways of working with each other, with ideas, and with materials and space have been studied and enriched over the past 30 years in the schools of Reggio Emilia through the interaction and collaboration of children, teachers, and parents. It we are serious about learning from this exceptional example of high-quality early childhood education, we too will be studying the Reggio Approach and developing our own versions of the highest-quality early education for many years to come.

One of my friends in the field says she feels the most valuable aspect of our investigation of the Reggio Approach has been the debate and intense dialogue that have ensued among teachers, professors of education, and parents of young children. We now find ourselves questioning and re-examining our practice at all levels. This has brought us out of what she calls "a rather satisfied complacency" and overall feeling that we were doing a good job, to an exciting new level of awareness of possibilities for growth and re-evaluation.

It seems to me one of the most important things for us to do is to examine and re-examine what fits for us. What about this approach seems remarkable, true, and achievable in this country? How can we adapt aspects of this approach in a way that they do not become just another trend in education that, like so many others, are dropped along the way because they are misunderstood? Can we develop a style of work in which we always consider how we might deepen our understanding of and respect for children, teachers, and parents in our daily practice?

As we in St. Louis, at the College School, at the St. Michael School, and at Clayton Schools' Family Center, search for answers and grow through our experience, we have made certain choices that we believe enrich the lives of children, teachers, and parents. We have visual artists on staff at two schools and one consulting regularly at the third school. We are convinced that materials presented in thoughtful ways offer infinite possibilities to children. We have a full-time pedagogical coordinator at one school and we recognize the importance of this role as we adapt it in our settings. We recognize and are learning new ways to support and challenge the extraordinary intelligence and creativity of young children. We know the importance of well-organized, beautiful classroom space and clearly presented communication of what children do and think as they learn. We have invited parents to be our partners in the education of their children and of ourselves, and they have accepted. As teachers, we are beginning to collaborate in ways we were unable to at first. We are embracing the idea that we are all responsible for what develops together. We are giving up our claim to our individual turf and singular opinions.

Some educators question whether what we have done is possible in public schools or in schools that do not have the network of support that we have in St. Louis. In addressing the public school issue, it is important to remember that Clayton Schools' Family Center is the early childhood component of a public school district that has always made early education a high priority.

It is true that a number of unusual advantages have supported our efforts in St. Louis, including my year of experience as an intern in the Diana and La Villetta Schools, 3 years of funding from a private foundation, and regular consulting help from Amelia Gambetti. It is also true that we never could have begun this effort without the commitment of a group of dedicated teachers who were willing to re-examine and reshape almost every aspect of their practice, or without the support of excellent institutions, both public and private, which wholeheartedly backed the initiative. We believe the commitment of teachers and the support of institutions are essential and that they are certainly within the reach of other schools.

Most educators who have tried, know that the work of change is hard and takes a long time. We in St. Louis have come to view our experience together as a journey. And we see that many early childhood educators in this country, and indeed all over the world, are traveling as well. We are all on the road together as we seek to provide children, teachers, and parents with the best possible experiences in school. To quote my colleagues in Vermont, Goldhaber, Smith, and Sortino (1997), "That is what we want too—to be on the road together. And perhaps to look back occasionally and reflect on and celebrate the distance we have covered and look forward to the challenges that await us" (p. 209).

If any of us in St. Louis, Missouri, or Burlington, Vermont, or any other place in the country are to move forward from here, we will need to continue to widen our lens and open our discussions. We must continue to make time to question everything we do and to consider many perspectives, including how aspects of this approach will grow and flourish for us in our American soil. We will have to continue to learn from and grow alongside parents. Finally, we will need to strengthen our growing capacity to see that children learn in extraordinary ways if we are able to observe them without blinders, provide them with rich experiences and materials, and grow and learn with them.

References

Badiner, A. (Ed.). (1990). *Dharma Gaia: A harvest of essays in Buddhism and ecology.* Berkeley, CA: Paralax Press.

Bettelheim, B. (1977). *The uses of enchantment.* New York: Vintage.

Brady, I. (1988). *The prayers of St. Francis.* Ann Arbor, MI: Servant Books.

Britton, J. (1992). *Language and learning.* London: Penguin.

Burton, J. (1980). Developing minds: The first visual symbols. *School Arts, 80*(2), 60–65.

Burton, J. (1991). Some basic considerations about "basic art." *Art Education, 44*(4), 34–41.

Burton, J., & Smith, N. R. (1978). *Materials and the structuring of experience: A method of curriculum design based on a theory of developmental interaction* [Consultation document]. Newton, MA: Newton Public Schools.

Cadwell, L. B., & Fyfe, B. V. (1997). Conversations with children. In J. Hendrick (Ed.), *First steps towards teaching the Reggio way* (pp. 84–98). Upper Saddle River, NJ: Prentice-Hall.

Cobb, E. (1977). *The ecology of imagination in childhood.* Dallas: Spring Publications.

College School of Webster Groves. (1994). [Brochure]. Webster Groves, MO: Author.

Department of Education, City of Reggio Emilia. (1990). *Cenni di storia* [An historical outline, data, and information]. Reggio Emilia, Italy: Center for Educational Research.

Donaldson, M. (1979). *Children's minds.* New York: Norton.

Duckworth, E. (1995). *The having of wonderful ideas* (2nd ed.). New York: Teachers College Press.

Edwards, C. (1993). Partner, nurturer, and guide: The roles of the Reggio teacher in action. In C. Edwards, L. Gandini, & G. Forman (Eds.), *The hundred languages of children: The Reggio Emilia approach to early childhood education* (pp. 151–170). Norwood, NJ: Ablex.

Edwards, C., Gandini, L., & Forman, G. (Eds.). (1993). *The hundred languages of children: The Reggio Emilia approach to early childhood education.* Norwood, NJ: Ablex.

Entsminger, V. (1994). *Teachers' perceptions of a pedagogic innovation: Barriers and mechanisms for successful implementation.* Unpublished doctoral dissertation, St. Louis University.

Forman, G., & Gandini, L. (Eds.). (1994). *The amusement park for birds* [video]. Amherst, MA: Performatics.

Fyfe, B. (1994). Images from the United States: Using ideas from the Reggio Emilia experience with American educators. In L. G. Katz & B. Cesarone (Eds.), *Reflections on the Reggio Emilia approach* (pp. 19–32). Urbana, IL: ERIC/EECE.

Fyfe, B. (1995). *Constructivism and documentation: The hundred languages of children.* Presentation at Bank Street College, New York.

Fyfe, B., & Cadwell, L. (1993). Bringing Reggio Emilia home. *Growing Times, 10*(3), 4–5. St. Louis.

Gandini, L. (1993). Fundamentals of the Reggio approach to early childhood education. *Young Children, 49*, 4–8.

Goldhaber, J., Smith, D., & Sortino, S. (1997). Observing, recording, understanding: The role of documentation in early childhood teacher education. In J. Hendrick (Ed.),

First steps toward teaching the Reggio way (pp. 197–209). Upper Saddle River, NJ: Prentice-Hall.

Greenman, J. (1988). *Caring spaces, learning places: Children's environments that work.* Redmond, WA: Exchange Press.

Hendrick, J. (Ed.). (1997). *First steps toward teaching the Reggio way.* Upper Saddle River, NJ: Prentice-Hall.

Jung, C. G. (1964). *Man and his symbols.* Garden City, NY: Doubleday.

Katz, L. G., & Cesarone, B. (Eds.). (1994). *Reflections on the Reggio Emilia approach.* Urbana, IL: ERIC/EECE.

Kellogg, R., & O'Dell, S. (1967). *The psychology of children's art.* New York: Random House.

Leopold, A. (1949). *A Sand County almanac.* New York: Oxford University Press.

Lewin, A. (1995). *The fundamentals of the Reggio approach.* Presentation to visiting delegation at the Model Early Learning Center, Washington, DC.

Lowenfeld, V. (1964). *Creative and mental growth.* New York: Macmillan.

Malaguzzi, L. (1992). *A message from Loris Malaguzzi* [video]. (L. Gandini, Trans.). Amherst, MA: Performanetics.

McLaughlin, M. (1995, May). Will Reggio Emilia change your child's preschool? *Working Mother,* 62–68.

Nelson, R. (1994). Identifying with the land. In P. Friederici (Ed.), *Proceedings of the 1994 forum: Writing and the natural world* (p. 10). Jamestown, NY: Roger Tory Peterson Institute of Natural History.

Rinaldi, C. (1992, January). *Corso d'aggiornamenti per nuovi insegnanti.* Address presented at Seminars for new teachers, Reggio Emilia, Italy.

Robertson, S. (1963). *Rose garden and labyrinth.* London: Routledge & Kegan Paul.

Rogoff, B. (1990). *Apprenticeship in thinking: Cognitive development in social context.* New York: Oxford University Press.

Rosen, H., & Rosen, C. (1974). *The language of primary school children.* Baltimore: Penguin.

Sanders, S. R. (1995). News of the wild. *Writing from the center* (pp. 116–120). Bloomington: Indiana University Press.

Smith, N., Fucigna, C., Kennedy, M., & Lord, L. (1993). *Experience and art: Teaching children to paint* (2nd Ed.). New York: Teachers College Press.

Snyder, G. (1979). *The practice of the wild.* New York: William Morrow.

Spaggiari, S. (1993). The community teacher partnership in the governance of the schools. In C. Edwards, L. Gandini, & G. Forman (Eds.), *The hundred languages of children: The Reggio Emilia approach to early childhood education* (pp. 91–99). Norwood, NJ: Ablex.

Thoreau, H. D. (1962). *Walden.* New York: Bantam Books. (Original work published 1854)

Udall, S. (1994). Introduction. In J. Sexton, *Listen to the trees* (p. 14). Boston: Bulfinch Press.

Vecchi, V. (1993). The role of the *Atelierista.* In C. Edwards, L. Gandini, & G. Forman (Eds.), *The hundred languages of children: The Reggio Emilia approach to early childhood education* (pp. 119–131). Norwood, NJ: Ablex.

Werner, H. (1948). *Comparative psychology of mental development.* New York: Science Editions.

Winkler, F. E. (1993). The wisdom of childhood. *Orion, 12*(2), 8–10.

Index

About the Author

Louise Boyd Cadwell lives in St. Louis, Missouri, where she is the *Atelierista* at the College School and consultant to the St. Michael School and Clayton School's Family Center. She returned to St. Louis after a one-year internship in the preschools of Reggio Emilia, Italy, where she worked with Italian educators to study the Reggio Approach to early childhood education. She continues to work with both Italian and American educators on the adaptation of the Reggio Approach in the United States. She received her Ph.D. in 1996 from the Union Institute. Her work as a teacher and researcher has focused on children's development through the arts and spoken and written language, particularly as children discover their place in the natural world.